RULES OF THUMB

A Guide for Writers

A Guide for Writers

SECOND EDITION

Jay Silverman
Nassau Community College

Elaine Hughes
Nassau Community College

Diana Roberts Wienbroer
Nassau Community College

McGraw-Hill, Inc.
New York   St. Louis   San Francisco   Auckland   Bogotá
Caracas   Lisbon   London   Madrid   Mexico   Milan
Montreal   New Delhi   Paris   San Juan   Singapore
Sydney   Tokyo   Toronto

RULES OF THUMB: A Guide for Writers

2 3 4 5 6 7 8 9 0   DOC   DOC   9 0 9 8 7 6 5 4 3

ISBN 0-07-057582-7
ISBN 0-07-057611-4 (Trade Edition)

This book was set in Palatino by J.M. Post Graphics, Corp.
The editors were Lesley Denton, Laurie PiSierra, and David Dunham.
The cover was designed by Merrill Haber.
R. R. Donnelley & Sons Company was printer and binder.

Library of Congress Cataloging-in-Publication Data

Silverman, Jay, (date).
   Rules of thumb: a guide for writers / Jay Silverman, Elaine Hughes, Diana Roberts Wienbroer.—2nd ed.
     p.   cm.
   Includes index.
   ISBN 0-07-057582-7
   1. English language—Rhetoric.   2. English language—Grammar—1950-   I. Hughes, Elaine.   II.   Wienbroer, Diana Roberts.
   III. Title.
PE1408.S4878   1993   92-26004
808'.042—dc20

To our students

ACKNOWLEDGMENTS

For their careful reading and questioning of various drafts of *Rules of Thumb*, we wish to thank Beverly Jensen; Polly Marshall, Hinds Community College; Nell Ann Pickett, Hinds Community College; and Larry Richman, Virginia Highlands Community College. Special thanks go to Sue Pohja, of Langenscheidt Publishers, Inc., whose enthusiasm for this book helped to create a trade edition.

We also appreciate the thoughtful comments of Andrew J. Auge, Loras College; Judy Bechtel, North Kentucky University; Robin Calitri, Merced College; Mimi Quen Cheikin, Nassau Community College; Diana Cox, Amarillo College; Ralph G. Dille, University of Southern Colorado; Kathryn Tripp Feldman, Nassau Community College; Ellen Gardiner, University of Mississippi; Bernice Kliman, Nassau Community College; Mary McFarland, Fresno City College; Kathy McHale, Nassau Community College; Bonnie Plumber, Eastern Kentucky University; Retta Porter, Hinds Community College; Sara L. Sanders, Coastal Community College; A. Gordon Van Ness III, Longwood College; and Dominick Yezzo, Nassau Community College.

We are grateful for the encouragement and enthusiasm of our colleagues in the English Department at Nassau Community College.

This book would not have existed but for our students—both as the audience we had in mind and as perceptive readers and critics.

CONTENTS

■ PART II: MEETING SPECIFIC ASSIGNMENTS 53

■ PART III: PUTTING A PAPER TOGETHER 89

■ PART IV: WRITING WITH ELEGANCE 115

HOW TO USE *RULES OF THUMB*

This book is for you if you love to write, but it's also for you if you *have* to write. *Rules of Thumb* is a quick reference guide that reduces each writing problem to a few practical points. You can use it easily, on your own, and feel confident in your writing.

We suggest that you read *Rules of Thumb* in small doses, out of order, when you need it. It's not like a novel that keeps you up late into the night. You'll need to read a few lines and then pause to see if you understand. After ten minutes, set the book aside. From time to time, look at the same points again as a reminder.

Part I, "Correctness," covers the most common mistakes. We put these rules first because they are what most students worry about and will want to have handy. However, when you are writing your ideas, don't get distracted with correctness; afterwards, take the time to look up the rules you need.

Part II, "Meeting Specific Assignments," offers help with writing under time pressure, as well as with writing literature papers and term papers.

Part III, "Putting a Paper Together," will help you with both content and style—if you're stuck, if you need to make a paper longer, or if you have trouble with introductions and conclusions.

Part IV, "Writing with Elegance," offers ways to grow as a writer.

You won't necessarily use these parts in order because the process of writing does not follow a set sequence. Generating ideas, organizing, revising, and correcting all happen at several points along the way.

Rules of Thumb doesn't attempt to cover every little detail of grammar and usage, but it does cover the most common problems we've seen as teachers of writing over the past twenty years. We chose the phrase "rules of thumb" because it means a quick guide. The top part of your thumb is roughly an inch long. Sometimes you need a ruler, marked in millimeters, but sometimes you can do fine by measuring with just your thumb. Your thumb takes only a second to use, and it's always with you. We hope you'll find *Rules of Thumb* just as easy and comfortable to use.

Jay Silverman
Elaine Hughes
Diana Roberts Wienbroer

RULES OF THUMB

A Guide for Writers

P A R T   O N E
CORRECTNESS

- A Word About Correctness
- Confusing Words
- One Word or Two?
- Spelling
- Abbreviations and Numbers
- Apostrophes
- Consistent Pronouns
- Correct Pronouns
- Vague Pronouns
- Sentence Fragments and Run-on Sentences
- Commas
- Semicolons and Colons
- Dashes and Parentheses
- Hyphens
- Quotation Marks
- Underlining or Quoting Titles
- Verb Agreement
- Shifting Verb Tenses
- Word Endings: *s* and *ed*
- Tangled Sentences

A WORD ABOUT CORRECTNESS

Too much concern about correctness can inhibit your writing; too little concern can come between you and your readers. Don't let the fear of errors dominate the experience of writing for you. On the other hand, we would be misleading you if we told you that correctness doesn't matter. Basic errors in writing will distract and turn off even the most determined readers. We encourage you to master these few rules as quickly as possible so that you can feel secure about your writing. Once that happens, you'll be free to concentrate on what you want to say.

CONFUSING WORDS

These words are used all the time, so you need to know them. Find the ones that give you trouble and learn those.

---

a
: Use before words starting with consonant sounds or long *u* (a bat, a cat, a union).

an
: Use before words starting with vowels or pronounced as if they did (an age, an egg, an hour, an M&M).

accept
: To take, to receive

    I never accept collect phone calls.

except
: Not including

    Everybody except Tina laughed.

affect
: To change or influence

    Starlight affects us in ways we don't understand.

effect
: The result, the consequence
    Effect is usually a noun, so you'll find *the* or *an* in front.

    We are studying the effects of starlight on human beings.

etc.
: Abbreviation of *et cetera*, which means "and so forth" in Latin. The *t* is in the middle. The *c* is at the end, followed by a period. Don't write *and etc.*

    We bought confetti, serpentine, fireworks, etc., for the party.

good, well	Test by trying your sentence with both. If *well* fits, use it.
	Leo plays third base well.
	Leo is a good third baseman.
	But note these tricky cases:
	Olivia looks good. (She's good-looking.)
	Rivka looks well. (She's no longer sick.)
	Clara sees well. (Her eyes work.)
it's	It is. Test by substituting *it is*.
	It's easy.
its	Possessive
	Every goat is attached to its own legs.
	No apostrophe. *It is* cannot be substituted.
lay	To put something down
	-ing: She is laying the cards on the table.
	Past Tense: He laid the cards on the table.
	Once you *lay* something down, it *lies* there.
lie	To recline
	I like to lie down in the afternoon.
	Past Tense (here's the tricky part): *lay*.
	Yesterday I lay down for half an hour.
	Lied always means "told a lie."
lying	Reclining
	He was lying down.
	Telling a lie
	She was lying to her boss.

loose	Not tight
	After he lost thirty pounds, his jeans were all loose.
lose	To misplace
	I constantly lose my glasses.
	To be defeated
	I win; you lose.
no, new, now, know, knew	*No* is negative; *new* is not old; *now* is the present moment. *Know* and *knew* refer to knowledge.
of, have	Remember: *could have, should have, would have*—or *would've*—not *would of*
passed	A course, a car, a football; also *passed away (died)*
	Kirtley passed me on the street; he also passed English. Saturday he passed for two touchdowns. The coach passed away.
past	Yesterdays (the past; past events); also, *beyond*
	He can never forget his past romances. You can't live in the past. Go two miles past the railroad tracks.
quiet	He is the quiet type.
quit	Sal quit her job the day she won the lottery.
quite	The monkeys are quite noisy today.

than	Comparison
	I'd rather dance than eat.
then	Next
	She then added a drop of water.
their	Something is theirs.
	You hurt their feelings.
there	*A place:* Go over there. *There* is . . . *There* are . . . *There* was . . . *There* were
	There are a thousand reasons why I fear her.
they're	They are.
	They're hard to handle.
to	*Direction:* Give it to me. Go to New York.
	A Verb Form: To see, to run, to be (Note that you barely pronounce *to*.)
too	*Very:* Too hot, too bad, too late, too much.
	Also: Me, too! (Note that you pronounce *too* clearly.)
two	2
were	*Past Tense:* You were, we were, they were.
we're	*We are:* We're as silly as we can be.
where	*A place:* Where were you?

whether	Not *weather*—rain or snow
	Tell me whether or not you love me.
who's·	*Who is:* Who's there? Who's coming with us?
whose	*Possessive:* Whose diamond is this?
women	Several of them.
	This woman is different from all other women.
	The Board was looking for a woman for the job.
	Don't write *a women.*
your	Belonging to you. Use only for your house, your car—*not* when you mean *you are.*
	That is your problem.
you're	You are.
	You're handsome.
	I'd like to know what you're thinking.

ONE WORD OR TWO?

If you can put another word between them, you'll know to keep them separate. Otherwise, you'll have to check them one by one.

a lot	I owe you a lot—a whole lot. (*A lot* is always written as two words.)
all ready	We were all ready for Grandpa's wedding.
already	Helen already has plans for Saturday.
all right	It's all right with me if you want to quit.
a long	Childhood seems like a long time.
along	Come along to the carnival.
a part	I want a part of the American pie.
apart	Even when we're apart, I think of you.
each other	Frankie and Johnny can't stand to be away from each other.
everybody	Everybody in the room danced frantically.
every day	It rains every day, every single day.
everyday	Fernando put on his everyday clothes.
every one	Bruce ate every one of the cookies—every last one.
everyone	Everyone likes pizza.
in depth	Study the biology textbook in depth.
in fact	In fact, Janine wasn't in the room when the ruckus started.
in order	In order to prove her point, Marty climbed onto the desk.
in spite of	I like you in spite of your churlish disposition.
intact	She's trying to keep her mind intact.
into	Ann Appleton fell into an easy job.

in touch	Please keep in touch with your sister.
itself	The cat sunned itself.
myself	I fixed the car myself.
nobody	Nobody knows how Mr. Avengail makes his money.
no one	No one ever calls me anymore.
nowadays	Nowadays, they call ice boxes "refrigerators."
nevertheless	Nevertheless, Billy's in for a tough campaign.
some time	I need some time alone.
sometimes	Sometimes I get the blues.
somehow	Somehow the laundry never gets done.
throughout	Throughout the entire summer, David lounged on the beach.
whenever	Whenever I hear that song, I start to cry.
whereas	I'm always on time, whereas my brother is always late.
wherever	Wherever Lillian goes, she goes in style.
withheld	Joe withheld the rent because the roof leaked.
without	You'll never catch Pearl without her sunglasses.

SPELLING

There's no getting around it. Correct spelling takes patience. But you can save time by learning the rules that fit your errors.

I *Before* E

Use *I* before *E*
Except after *C*
Or when sounded like *A*
As in *neighbor* and *weigh*.

believe	deceive	freight
friend	receive	vein
piece	conceit	

Exceptions:

weird   foreign   leisure   seize   their

Word Endings

- The quiet -*ed* endings: three -*ed* endings are not always pronounced clearly, but they need to be written.

  used to
  supposed to
  prejudiced

- -*sk* and -*st* endings: when *s* is added to words like these, it isn't always pronounced, but it still needs to be there.

asks	consists	psychologists
risks	insists	scientists
desks	suggests	terrorists

- The -*y* endings:

  When a verb ends in *y*, keep the *y* when you add *ing*. To add *s* or *ed*, change the *y* to *i*.

crying	cries	cried
studying	studies	studied
trying	tries	tried

  When a noun ends in *y*, make it plural by changing the *y* to *i* and adding *es*.

activities	families	theories

  Exception: Simply add *s* to nouns ending in *ey*.

attorneys	monkeys	valleys

- *p* or *pp*? *t* or *tt*?

  Listen to the *vowel before* the added part. If the vowel sounds like its own letter name, *use only one consonant:*

  writer   writing

  The *i* sounds like the name of the letter *i*, so you use one *t*.

  If the vowel before the added part has a different sound from its name, *double the consonant:*

  written

  The *i* sounds like the *i* in *it*, so you double the *t*.

  The same method works for *hoping* and *hopping*. Listen for the different sounds of the letter *o*.

  Here are some other examples:

beginning	dropping	quitting
stopped	occurred	referred

  An exception: coming

Words with Prefixes and Suffixes

When you add a prefix or suffix, you usually keep the spelling of the root word.

*mis*spell	sudden*ness*	*dis*satisfaction
hope*ful*	*dis*appear	govern*ment*
*un*noticed	environ*ment*	

The *-ly* endings also follow this rule.

really   totally   lonely   finally

But *truly* does not follow the rule.

Exception: The final *e* is usually dropped before a suffix that starts with a vowel.

debat*able*	sensi*ble*
lov*able*	

Tricky Words

Look hard at the middle of each word:

de*fini*tely	pro*ba*bly
se*pa*rate	in*te*rest
re*peti*tion	us*ua*lly
o*pin*ion	ne*ces*sary
em*bar*rass	fam*ili*ar
acco*mmo*date	

Tips for Becoming a Better Speller

- Keep an on-going list of every word you misspell. Study the list once a week.
- Write any word you misspell three times and then add it to your list.
- Sound out words. Use your hearing to help you spell words syllable by syllable.
- Make a habit of using your dictionary.

ABBREVIATIONS AND NUMBERS

When in doubt, spell it out.

■ ABBREVIATIONS

- As a general rule, don't abbreviate—especially don't use abbreviations like these in papers:

dept.	yr.	NY	Eng.	Thurs.
w/o	co.	&	gov't.	Prof.

- But do abbreviate words which you *always* see abbreviated—such as certain titles with proper names and well-known organizations:

Mr. Smith	FBI
St. Bartholomew	IBM

- Abbreviate Dr. *only* before a name:

The doctor	Dr. Salk

■ NUMBERS

Spell Out

- Numbers that take only one or two words

  nine   twenty-seven   two billion

- Numbers that begin a sentence

  One hundred four years ago the ship sank.
  The ship sank 104 years ago.

- Numbers that form a compound word

  a two-year-old baby

- Fractions

  one-half

15

Use Numerals for

- Numbers that require three or more words

  1,889   162

- Dates, page references, room numbers, statistics, addresses, percentages, and dollars and cents

1889	7,500 residents	99.44%
page 2	221 B Baker Street	$5.98

- A list or series of numbers

  1, 4, 9, 16, 25
  seats 12, 14, and 16

APOSTROPHES

Most of the time, when you add an *s* to a word, you don't need an apostrophe. Use apostrophes for contractions and possessives.

Do Not Add an Apostrophe; Just Add s *or* es

- To make a plural

  Two bosses   Three dogs   Five shoes

- To a present-tense verb

  He sees.   She says.

  Look hard at *sees* and *says:* no apostrophe.

  It talks.   Rain falls.   Carol sings.

Add an Apostrophe

- To a contraction (put the apostrophe where the missing letter was)

doesn't = does not	it's = it is	that's
don't	I'm	weren't
didn't	you're	what's

- To a possessive

John's hat	men's room	a night's sleep
Ms. Jones's opinion	women's room	today's world
Baldwin's sentences	people's feelings	

  If the word is plural and already ends with *s*, just add an apostrophe after the *s*.

  my friends' apartment (several friends)

  But note: Pronouns in possessive form have *no* apostrophe.

  its   hers   his   ours   theirs   yours   **17**

- To the plural of a letter or a word out of context

  Sonia made all *A*'s last fall
  That last paragraph had five *really*'s in it.

  Note that the letter or word is italicized (or underlined).

CONSISTENT PRONOUNS

Make a conscious choice of your pronouns. Don't shift from *a person* to *they* to *you* to *I*.

Avoid writing sentences like

I got mad; it does make you feel upset when people don't listen.

or

A young person has to be diligent if they want to get ahead.

Here are the choices:

a person someone	These words can lead to awkward writing and create errors. If a person is strong, they will stand up for themselves. I know someone rich, and they are not very happy. Note that *a person* and *someone* are singular; *they* is plural. Instead of *a person* or *someone,* use *people* (which fits with *they*). If people are strong, they will stand up for themselves. Or, better yet, use a true-to-life example, a real person: My cousin Marc is strong: he stands up for himself. A real example not only makes the grammar correct, but it is also much more interesting and memorable. *A person* and *someone* are nobodies.
he he or she	The old-fashioned choice to go with *a person* would be *he*: If a person is strong, he will stand up for himself.

19

But this choice presumes that *a person* is male. It should be avoided because it is sexist language. *He or she* is possible, but not if it comes several times in a row; *He or she,* when repeated, becomes clunky and awkward.

If a person is strong, he or she will stand up for himself or herself whenever he or she can.

Avoid *he/she* and *s/he.* The best solution, usually, is to use plurals such as *people* and *they.*

Strong people stand up for themselves.

I   Don't be afraid of *I.* It is very strong in writing about emotions and experience. In these matters, being *objective* is not as good as being *truthful.* As Thoreau says, "I should not talk so much about myself if there were anybody else whom I knew as well." You don't, however, need phrases like *I think* or *in my opinion* because the whole paper is, after all, what *you* choose to say.

you   *You* is good for giving directions and writing letters. For essays, it may seem too informal or too preachy.

If you're strong, you stand up for yourself.

Try *we* instead, when you mean *people in general.*

If we are strong, we stand up for ourselves.

In any case, beware of mixing pronouns.

Riding my bicycle is good for your legs.

one   *One* means *a person*—singular. If you use it, you must stick with it:

If one is strong, one stands up for oneself.

One is an option for solving the *he/she* problem; it is appropriate for formal writing. Nevertheless, when repeated, *one* can sound stuffy. How many times can one say *one* before one makes oneself sound silly?

we

We can be used to mean *people in general.*

If we are strong, we stand up for our rights.

Be careful that you mean more than just yourself. Using *I* might be more appropriate.

they

They is the best solution to the *he/she* problem, but remember that *they* must refer to a plural, such as *many people* or *some people.*

If people are strong, they stand up for themselves.

Note: Use *themselves;* do not use *themself.*

no pronoun

Often you can avoid the problem entirely. Instead of

A young person has to be diligent if he or she wants to get ahead.

write:

A young person has to be diligent to get ahead.

CORRECT PRONOUNS (*I* VS. *ME*)

I, she, he, we, they, and *who* identify the persons doing the action. *Me, her, him, us, them,* and *whom* identify the persons receiving the action.

Pairs: *My friends and I* / *My friends and me*

With a pair of people, try the sentence without the other person:

My friends and *I* went to the movies.
(. . . I went to the movies, *not* Me went to the movies.)

Carter gave the tickets to my friends and me.
(Carter gave the tickets to me, *not* to I.)

The same rule goes for *him, her, he, she.*

We sued her father and her.
(We sued her, *not* We sued she.)

Note: Put yourself last in a list:

My friends and I . . .
Beverly gave pumpkin cake to Noah and me.

Don't be afraid of *me;* it's often right.

Between you and me, Mickey is heading for a fall.
(*Not* Between you and I.)

Don't use *myself* when *me* will do.

Sam did the typing for Toby and me.
(*Not* . . . for Toby and myself.)

Comparisons

Use *I, he, she, we, they* when comparing with the subject of the sentence—usually the first person in the sentence.

Phil was kinder to Sarah than I was.
John is sweeter than she is.

Sometimes *is* is left off the end:

John is sweeter than she.

Use *me, him, her, us, them* when comparing with the receiver, the object of the sentence—usually the person mentioned later in the sentence.

Phil was kinder to Sarah than to me.

Note the difference:

He was nastier to Ramona than I. (He was nastier to Ramona than I was.)
He was nastier to Ramona than me. (He was nastier to Ramona than to me.)

Who/Whom

Use *whom* after prepositions (to whom, of whom, for whom, from whom, with whom).

For whom were these roses intended?

Use *who* for subjects of verbs.

Who should I say is calling?

When in doubt, use *who*.

VAGUE PRONOUNS

Certain pronouns—*which, it, this, that,* and *who*—must refer to a single word, not to a whole phrase.

Which

Which causes the most trouble of the five. Don't overuse it.

Imprecise: Last week I felt sick in which I didn't even get to go to school.

Precise: Last week I felt sick. I didn't even get to go to school.

Precise: Last week I had a cold which kept me from going to school.

In the last example, *which* clearly refers to *cold.*

Use *in which* only when you mean that one thing is inside the other:

The box in which I keep my jewelry fell apart.

It

When you use *it,* make sure the reader knows what *it* is. *It* is often weak at the start of a sentence when *it* refers to nothing.

Imprecise: Eleanore ate a big Chinese dinner and then had a chocolate milkshake for dessert. *It* made her sick.

Precise: Eleanore ate a big Chinese dinner and then had a chocolate milkshake for dessert. The combination made her sick.

This

This cannot refer to a whole situation or a group of things, so insert a word after *this* to sum up what *this* refers to.

Imprecise: She never calls me, she's never ready when I pick her up for a date, and she forgot my birthday. This makes me angry.

Precise: She never calls me, she's never ready when I pick her up for a date, and she forgot my birthday. This neglect makes me angry.

That

That refers to things.

The car that I bought Wednesday is already in the shop.

Who

Use *who* for people—not *which*.

The runner who finished last got all the publicity.

SENTENCE FRAGMENTS AND RUN-ON SENTENCES

To correct both sentence fragments and run-on sentences, you need to know what a complete sentence is.

Often you reach a pause in your writing, and you wonder, "Do I put a comma or a period?" The length of a sentence has nothing to do with the right choice. You need to look at what comes before and after the punctuation. Here is a system for recognizing complete sentences, sentence fragments, and run-on sentences.

■ RECOGNIZING COMPLETE SENTENCES

- A sentence always has a *subject* and a *verb*:

  I won.
  Phillippe snores.
  This soup is cold.

  I, Phillippe, soup are the subjects; *won, snores, is* are the verbs. Notice that the verb enables the subject to *do* or *be* something.

  These very short sentences have only a one-word subject and a one-word verb.

- Sentences can have more than one subject and more than one verb:

  Tracy and Pete have a new home.
  They bought an old house and restored it.

- Sometimes the subject is understood to be "you," the reader; the sentence is usually a command or a direction:

  Avoid submerging this product in water.
  Walk two blocks past the traffic light.

- Usually a word or phrase completes the subject and verb:

  Janeen walks three miles a day.
  Suzanne spent all of her savings.

Grasshoppers are lazy.
This is my latest fiancé.

Variations

- Sometimes a word or group of words introduces the main part of a sentence:

  However, the bar is closed.
  Therefore, we are planning a trip to the moon.
  For example, Mona screams when she talks.
  Then we drove a thousand miles.
  At the end of the game, the umpire and the pitcher got into a fight.
  In the cabin by the lake, you'll find the paddles and life jackets.

- Sometimes two short complete sentences are joined by a comma and connecting word or by a semicolon:

  Janeen walks three miles a day, but she still eats junk food.
  Suzanne spent all of her savings, and now she has to start using her credit cards.
  Grasshoppers are lazy; they are not very hard to catch.

- Sometimes a sentence has two parts—the main part (a complete short sentence) and a *subordinated* part (a complete short sentence preceded by a *subordinating* word, such as *because, although, if, when, after,* and *while*).

  I feed my snakes when I get home.
  Suzanne spent all of her savings because her brother is ill.

Notice in the first sentence that "I feed my snakes" could be a complete sentence. On the other hand, "when I get home" is not complete by itself. In the second sentence, "because her brother is ill" is also incomplete if used by itself.

The two parts of each sentence are reversible:

When I get home, I feed my snakes.
Because her brother is ill, Suzanne spent all of her savings.

■ RECOGNIZING SENTENCE FRAGMENTS

Many sentence fragments may appear to be complete sentences, but they have elements that make them incomplete.

- A subordinating word in front of a sentence creates a fragment:

Fragment: Although Janeen walks three miles a day.

You can fix this fragment by dropping the subordinating word or by connecting the fragment to the sentence before or after it.

Correct Sentences: Janeen walks three miles a day.
Although Janeen walks three miles a day, she still has to watch her diet.
Janeen still has to watch her diet although she walks three miles a day.

Here are the most common subordinating words; they always start the incomplete part of a sentence:

when	if
before	because
after	although (even though)
as	unless
while	whereas

A subtle point: Watch out for *and.* Putting *and* between a fragment and a sentence doesn't fix the fragment.

Still a Fragment: Although Janeen walks three miles a day and she still watches her diet.

Correct Sentence: Although Janeen walks three miles a day and she still watches her diet, she has not yet reached her goal.

- Certain verb forms cannot serve as the main verb of a sentence:

Watch out for verbs ending in *ing*.

Incorrect: The boys ran toward the ocean. Leaping across the hot sand.
I have three good friends. One being my cousin.
I love walking in the evening and taking in nature's beauty. The sun setting over the prairie. The wind blowing the tall grass.

One solution is to connect the fragment to the preceding sentence.

Correct: The boys ran toward the ocean, leaping across the hot sand.
I love walking in the evening and taking in nature's beauty—the sun setting over the prairie and the wind blowing the tall grass.

The second solution is to change the *-ing* verb to a complete verb.

Correct: They leaped across the hot sand.
One is my cousin.

To verbs (*to be, to feel*) also frequently begin fragments.

Incorrect: I went back home to talk to my father. To tell him how I feel.
Keep this hairdryer away from the sink. To avoid submersion in water

Fix these fragments by connecting them to the sentence before or after or by adding a subject and verb:

Correct: I went back home to talk to my father, to tell him how I feel.
I went back home to talk to my father. I needed to tell him how I feel.
Keep this hairdryer away from the sink to avoid submersion in water.
Keep this hairdryer away from the sink. You must avoid submerging it in water.

To verbs and *-ing* verbs *can* begin sentences if a complete verb comes later.

Correct: Leaping across the hot sand hurts my feet.
             To talk to my father always calms me down.

- A repeated word can create a fragment.

Incorrect: Elizabeth's the ideal cat. A cat who both plays and
               purrs.
               I am tired of this. Tired of waking up to rain every
               day.

The best solution here is to replace the period with a comma.

Correct: Elizabeth's the ideal cat, a cat who both plays and
             purrs.
             I am tired of this, tired of waking up to rain every
             day.

- You will notice that professional writers sometimes use sentence fragments for emphasis or style. Be sure you have control over fragments before you experiment. In the right spot, fragments can be very strong.

A Checklist for Recognizing Sentence Fragments

Check sentences that start with subordinating words.

Check sentences with *to* or *-ing* verbs.

Check for the repetition of a word from the end of the previous sentence.

Check for these words, which rarely begin sentences:

such as	which	
especially	who	
not	whose	except in a question
like, just like	how	
the same as	what	

■ RECOGNIZING RUN-ON SENTENCES

A run-on sentence happens when you have two complete sentences, but you have only a comma or no punctuation between them.

Run-on: I went to Gorman's Ice Cream Parlor, I ordered a triple hot fudge sundae.

Run-on: Suzanne spent all of her savings now she is flat broke.

There are four ways to fix a run-on:

● Put a period between the two sentences:

> I went to Gorman's Ice Cream Parlor. I ordered a triple hot fudge sundae.
> Suzanne spent all of her savings. Now she is flat broke.

● Put a semicolon between the two sentences:

> I went to Gorman's Ice Cream Parlor; I ordered a triple hot fudge sundae.
> Suzanne spent all of her savings; now she is flat broke.

● Put a comma and a conjunction between the two sentences. The conjunctions are *and, but, so, yet, for, or,* and *nor.*

> I went to Gorman's Ice Cream Parlor, and I ordered a triple hot fudge sundae.
> Suzanne spent all of her savings, so now she is flat broke.

● Use a subordinating word with one of the sentences:

> I went to Gorman's Ice Cream Parlor, where I ordered a triple hot fudge sundae.
> Because Suzanne spent all of her savings, now she is flat broke.

The two most common spots where run-ons occur are

● When a pronoun begins the second sentence:

> Tabby was running around the yard. She fell into a hole.
> The light floated toward us. It gave an eerie glow.

Note that *she* and *it* begin new sentences.

- When *however* begins the second sentence:

  She says she loves me. However, she doesn't show it.

  However and *although* are often used with similar meaning, but they need different punctuation:

  Suzanne spent all of her savings. However, her rich aunt is
  helping her out.
  Suzanne spent all of her savings although she didn't buy
  anything excessive.

COMMAS

You don't need a comma
every time you breathe.
Here are four places
you need them.

- Put a comma before *and, but, so, yet, or, for,* and *nor*
  when they connect two sentences.

  The roads are slick, but you can make it.
  Gina intended to win the weight-lifting pageant, and that's
    exactly what she did.
  They called me in for a job interview, so I had to get new
    shoes.
  Not only did Melva run a restaurant, but she also wrote a
    cookbook.

  However, don't automatically stick in a comma just
  because a sentence is long.

  The short man smoking a cigar and shouting at the hostess is
    my uncle Jules.

- Use commas between parts of a series of three or more.

  I bought Perrier, Wheat Thins, and Velveeta for my party.
  Diamond climbed up the ladder, marched to the end of the
    diving board, took a big spring, and came down in a belly
    bust.

  In the class sat a bearded man, a police officer, a woman
    eating a sandwich, and a parakeet.

  (Without the comma, what happens to the parakeet?

  Don't use a comma in a pair.

  I bought Perrier and Velveeta.
  Curt and Rixana are joining us this afternoon and going for a
    boat ride.
  Mary Ellen's mother handed out hard candies and made us sit
    while she played the piano.

- Use a comma after an introductory part of a sentence.

  However, Kathryn proved him wrong.
  For example, Larry built his own house.
  If we had left on time, we would be there by now.
  After we got home, she gave me a cup of that terrible herb tea.
  When James walked in, the whole family was laughing
    hysterically.

- Surround an insertion or interruption with a *pair* of commas.

  My cousin, who thinks she is always right, was dead wrong.
  Billy, of course, won the election.
  Scooby Doo, the Pekinese, has a cold.
  If you want to go with me, Emilio, you'd better hurry up.
  Milton, even though no one invited him, arrived first at the party.

These are wrong if you use only one comma.

Places and *dates* are treated as insertions. Note especially that commas surround the year and the state.

The hospital was in Oshkosh, Wisconsin, not far from Omro.
I was born on August 15, 1954, at seven in the morning.

SEMICOLONS AND COLONS

Semicolons can be used instead of periods; they also can separate parts of a complicated list. Colons create suspense: they set up a list, a quotation, or an emphatic statement.

■ SEMICOLONS

- Use a semicolon to connect two related sentences; each half must be a complete sentence.

  He was fat; she was thin.
  Hope for the best; plan for the worst.
  I'll never forget the day of the circus; that's when I met the trapeze artist who changed my life.

  A semicolon usually comes before certain transition words; a comma follows the transition.

however	therefore	otherwise
nevertheless	in other words	instead
for example	on the other hand	meanwhile
besides	furthermore	unfortunately

  Schubert was a great composer; however, Beethoven was greater.
  The bank lost two of my deposits; therefore, I am closing my account.

  Semicolons are best used to emphasize a strong connection between the two sentences.

- Use semicolons instead of commas in a list when some of the parts already have commas.

  To make it as an actor, you need, first of all, some natural talent; second, the habits of discipline and concentration; and third, the ability to promote yourself.

■ COLONS

Use a colon after a complete sentence to introduce related details.

Before a colon you must have a *complete statement*. Don't use a colon after *are* or *include* or *such as*.

Colons can introduce

● A list

I came home loaded with supplies: a tent, a sleeping bag, and a pack.

● A quotation

The author begins with a shocker: "Mother spent her summer sitting naked on a rock."

● An example

I love to eat legumes: for example, beans or lentils.

● An emphatic assertion

This is the bottom line: I refuse to work for only $5.00 an hour.

Use a colon before a subtitle.

Pablo Picasso: The Playful Artist

When you type, leave two spaces after a colon.

DASHES AND PARENTHESES

Dashes and parentheses separate a word or remark from the rest of the sentence.

■ DASHES

Dashes highlight the part of the sentence they separate, or show an abrupt change of thought in mid-sentence, or connect a fragment to a sentence.

Alberta Hunter—still singing at the age of eighty—performed nightly at The Cookery in New York City.
At night the forest is magical and fascinating—and yet it terrifies me.
Living the high life—that's what I want.

Dashes are very handy; they can replace a period, comma, colon, or semicolon. However, they are usually informal, so don't use many—or you will seem to have dashed off your paper.

When you type, two hyphens make a dash; do not space before or after the dash.

■ PARENTHESES

Parentheses de-emphasize the words they separate. Use them to enclose brief explanations or interruptions. They can contain either part of a sentence or a whole sentence.

I demanded a reasonable sum ($10.50 an hour), and they met my request.
Polly's last movie disappointed both fans and critics. (See the attached reviews.)
Mayme drives slowly (she claims her car won't go over 40 miles per hour), so she gets tickets for causing traffic jams.

- Put any necessary punctuation *after* the second parenthesis if the parentheses contain part of a sentence.

37

- If the parentheses contain a complete sentence, put the period *inside* the second parenthesis. Notice, however, that you don't capitalize or use a period when parentheses enclose a sentence within a sentence.

Be sparing with parentheses. Too many can chop up your sentences.

HYPHENS

Hyphens are used to join two words or to divide a word at the end of the line.

Hyphens join compound words.

    self-employed
    in-laws
    seventy-five

Hyphens make a two-word adjective before a noun, but not after it.

    Maggie has a high-paying job.
    Maggie's job is high paying.

    George Eliot was a nineteenth-century author.
    George Eliot's prose is recognizably nineteenth century.

A hyphen can divide a multisyllable word at the end of a line. Divide only long words and only between syllables. When in doubt, do not divide.

In typing, use two hyphens to make a dash.

QUOTATION MARKS

Use quotation marks any time you use someone else's exact words. If they are not the exact words, don't surround them with quotation marks.

Punctuation Before a Quotation

Here are three ways to lead into a quotation:

- For short quotations (a word or a phrase), don't say *Twain says,* and don't put a comma before the quotation. Simply use the writer's phrase as it fits smoothly into your sentence:

  Huck Finn finds it "lovely" to float down the Mississippi River on a raft.

- Put a comma before the quotation marks if you use *he says.* Put no comma if you use *he says that.*

  Mark Twain says, "It's lovely to live on a raft."
  Mark Twain says that "It's lovely to live on a raft."

- Use a colon (:) before a quotation of a sentence or more. Be sure you have a compete statement before the colon. Don't use *he says.*

  Twain romanticizes Huck's life on the river: "It's lovely to live on a raft."

Punctuation After a Quotation

At the end of a quotation, the period or comma goes *inside* the quotation marks. Do not close the quotation marks until the person's words end.

Twain writes, ". . . you could hear a fiddle or a song coming over from one of them crafts. It's lovely to live on a raft."

Semicolons go outside of closing quotation marks.

Huck says, "It's lovely to live on a raft"; however, this raft
eventually drifts him into trouble.

Question marks and exclamation marks go inside if the
person is asking or exclaiming. (If *you* are asking or
exclaiming, the mark goes outside.)

"Have you read *Huckleberry Finn?*" she asked.
Did Twain call Huck's life "lovely"?

When your quotation is more than a few words, let the
quotation end your sentence. Otherwise you're liable to
get a tangled sentence.

Tangled: Huck says, "It's lovely to live on a raft" illustrates his
love for freedom.

Correct: Huck says, "It's lovely to live on a raft." This quotation
illustrates his love for freedom.

Indenting Long Quotations

Long quotations (three or more lines) do not get quotation
marks. Instead, start on a new line and indent the whole
quotation ten spaces from the left margin. After the
quotation, return to the original margin and continue your
paragraph.

Huck and Jim lead a life of ease:
> Sometimes we'd have the whole river all to ourselves
> for the longest time. Yonder was the banks and the
> islands, across the water; and maybe a spark—which
> was a candle in a cabin window—and sometimes on the
> water you could see a spark or two—on a raft or a
> scow, you know; and maybe you could hear a fiddle or
> a song coming over from one of them crafts. It's lovely
> to live on a raft.

An ellipsis (. . .) means words are left out. Brackets ([ ])
mean you've added or changed a word to make the
quotation clear.

Sometimes we'd have that whole river [the Mississippi] all to
  ourselves for the longest time. . . . It's lovely to live on a raft.

Note that the fourth dot with an ellipsis is a period.

Dialogue

In dialogue, start a new paragraph every time you switch
from one speaker to the other.

"Did you enjoy reading *Huckleberry Finn?*" asked Professor
Migliaccio.
"I guess so," Joylene said, "but the grammar is awful."
The professor thought a moment. "You know, the book was
once banned in Boston because of that. I guess Twain's
experiment still has some shock value."
"Well, it shocked me," said Joylene. "I'd like to know why he
wrote it that way."

Writing About a Word or Phrase

When you discuss a word or phrase, surround it with
quotation marks.

Advertisers use "America," while news reporters refer to "the
  United States."
The name "Mark Twain" means "two fathoms deep."

Do not use quotation marks around slang; either use the
word without quotation marks or find a better word.

Quotation Within a Quotation

For quotations within a quotation, use single quotation marks:

According to radio announcer Rhingo Lake, "The jockey clearly screamed 'I've been foiled!' as the horse fell to the ground right before the finish line."

Quoting Poetry

For poetry, when quoting two or more lines, indent ten spaces from the left margin and copy the lines of poetry exactly as the poet arranged them.

> We are such stuff
> As dreams are made on; and our little life
> Is rounded with a sleep.

When quoting a *few* words of poetry that include a line break, use a slash mark to show where the poet's line ends.

In *The Tempest*, Shakespeare calls us "such stuff/ As dreams are made on. . . ."

UNDERLINING OR QUOTING TITLES

Underline titles of longer works and use quotation marks for titles of shorter works.

- <u>Underline</u> titles of longer works, such as books, magazines, plays, newspapers, movies, and television shows.

  <u>Newsweek</u>   <u>Saturday Night Live</u>
  <u>The New York Times</u>   <u>The Wizard of Oz</u>
  <u>War and Peace</u>   <u>Hamlet</u>

  Underlining indicates italics to the printer. Some word processors allow you to use italics instead of underlining.

- Put quotation marks around titles of shorter works, such as short stories, articles, poems, songs, and chapter titles.

  "Little Miss Muffet"
  "The Star-Spangled Banner"
  "The Pit and the Pendulum"

  Note: Capitalize only the first word and all major words in a title.

- Do not underline or place quotation marks around your title on a cover sheet—unless your title contains someone else's title:

  My Week on a Shrimp Boat
  An Analysis of Frost's "Fire and Ice"
  The Vision of War in <u>The Red Badge of Courage</u>

VERB AGREEMENT

The word before the verb is not always its subject. Look for *who* or *what* is doing the action.

- Remember that two singular subjects joined by *and* (the bird and the bee) make a plural and need a plural verb.

  The bird and the bee make music together.

- Sometimes an insertion separates the subject and verb.

  The drummer, not the other musicians, sets the rhythm.
  The lady who sells flowers has a mysterious voice.

- Sometimes an *of* phrase separates the subject and verb; read the sentence without the *of* phrase.

  One of the guests is a sleepwalker.
  Each of us owns a Wurlitzer juke box.
  The use of cigarettes is dangerous.

- The subject of the sentence follows *there was, there were, there is, there are.*

  There was one cow in the entire field.
  There were two cows in the back yard.

- Words with *one* and *body* are singular.

  Everyone except for the twins was laughing.
  Somebody always overheats the copying machine.

- Sometimes a group can be singular.

  My family eats crowder peas.
  The team argues after every game.
  A thousand dollars is a lot of money to carry around.

- *-ing* phrases are usually singular.

  Dating two people is tricky.

SHIFTING VERB TENSES

Often you find yourself slipping back and forth between present and past verb tenses. Be consistent, especially within each paragraph.

Use the present tense for writing about literature.

Scarlett comes into the room and pulls down the draperies.
Hamlet feels sorry for himself.

Use the simple past tense to tell your own stories or stories from history.

I lied to the Assistant Principal.
President Truman waved after he boarded the train.

had

Watch out for *had:* You often don't need it. Use *had* to refer to events that were already finished when your story or example took place—the past before the past that you're describing. To check, try adding *previously* or *already* next to *had*.

In 1986, we moved to New York. We had lived in Florida for three years.
If I had known that the wheel was loose, I would have stopped.

would

Most of the time, you can leave out *would*. Use it for something that happened regularly during a period of the past.

The teacher would always make us stand up when she entered the room.

Use *would* for hypothetical situations.

If I were you, I would apologize right now.

could can	Use *could* to refer to the past and *can* to refer to the present.

> *Past:* Frank couldn't go in the ocean because it was too rough.

> *Present:* Frank can't swim in the ocean because it's too rough.

Use *could* to show what might happen and doesn't; use *can* to show ability.

My parents make good money. They *could* buy us anything, but they don't.
My parents make good money. They *can* buy us anything we want.

gone eaten done seen written	Avoid expressions such as *I seen* and *He has went*. Use *gone, eaten, done, seen, written* after a helping verb.

We went.	We have gone.
I ate.	I have eaten.
He did it.	He has done it.
He saw the light.	He has seen the light.
She wrote well.	She has written a play.

WORD ENDINGS: S AND ED

If word endings give you problems, train yourself to check every noun to see if it needs s and every verb to see if it needs s or ed.

Add ed

- To form most simple past tenses

  She walked.   He tripped.   Mae asked a question.

- After *has, have, had*

  He has walked.   We have talked.   She had already arrived.

- After the *be* verbs *(are, were, is, was, am, be, been, being)*

  They are prejudiced.   She was depressed.   He will be prepared.

Do Not Add ed

- After *to*   He loved to walk.

- After *would*   Every day he would walk three miles.

- After *did, didn't*   He didn't walk very often.

- After an irregular past tense   I bought bread.
                                                He found his keys.
                                                The cup fell.

Add s

- To form a plural (more than one)

  many scientists   two potatoes

- To the present tense of a verb that follows *he, she, it,* or a singular noun

  He walks.   It talks.
  She says.   The dog sees the fire hydrant.
  Bill asks.   Polly insists.

Note: Usually when there is an *s* on the noun, there is no *s* on the verb.

Pots rattle.	A pot rattles.
The candles burn swiftly.	The candle burns swiftly.

● To form a possessive (with an apostrophe):

John's mother	today's society
Sally's house	women's clothing

Do Not Add s *to a Verb*

● If there is an *s* on the subject of the sentence or if there are two subjects

Tulips come from Holland.
Salt and sugar look the same.

● If one of these helping verbs comes before the main verb

does	may	will	shall	can
must	might	would	should	could

Kenneth should clean out the back seat of his car.
Angelica can get there in thirty minutes.

TANGLED SENTENCES

Look at your sentences to make sure the parts go with each other.

■ PARALLEL STRUCTURE

The parts of a list (or pair) must be in the same format.

Not Parallel: I love swimming, to play tennis, and baseball.

Parallel: I love swimming, tennis, and baseball.

Parallel: I love to swim, to play tennis, and to play baseball.

Not Parallel: To reach the camp, Marty paddled a canoe and then a horse.

Parallel: To reach the camp, Marty paddled a canoe and then rode a horse.

■ DANGLERS

There are two problems. In one, a word (often a pronoun) has been left out, so that the introductory phrase doesn't fit with what follows.

Dangler: Dashing wildly across the platform, the subway pulled out of the station.
(This sounds as if the subway dashed across the platform. To correct it, add the missing word— in this case, *we.*)

Correct: Dashing wildly across the platform, we saw the subway pull out of the station.

Correct: As we dashed wildly across the platform, the subway pulled out of the station.

50

The second problem occurs when a phrase or word in a sentence is too far from the part it goes with.

Dangler: A former athlete, the reporters interviewed Terrence Harley about the use of steroids.

(This sounds as if the reporters are a former athlete.)

Correct: The reporters interviewed Terrence Harley, a former athlete, about the use of steroids.

■ MIXED SENTENCE PATTERNS

Sometimes you start with one way of getting to a point, but one of the words slides you into a different way of saying it. The two patterns get mixed up. Correct a mixed sentence pattern by using one pattern or the other.

Mixed (Incorrect):   By opening the window lets in fresh air. (Here the writer started to say "By opening the window, I let in fresh air," but the phrase *opening the window* took over.)

Correct: By opening the window, I let in fresh air.

Correct: Opening the window lets in fresh air.

Read your sentence as a whole to make sure that the end goes with the beginning.

Mixed (Incorrect):   In the Republic of Cameroon has over two hundred local languages.

Correct: The Republic of Cameroon has over two hundred local languages.

Correct: In the Republic of Cameroon, over two hundred local languages are spoken.

PART TWO

MEETING SPECIFIC ASSIGNMENTS

- Format of College Papers
- Writing in Class
- Using the College Library
- Writing About Literature
- How to Quote from Your Sources
- Writing Research Papers
- Plagiarism (Cheating)
- Documentation

FORMAT OF COLLEGE PAPERS

■ TYPING YOUR PAPER

Paper

- Use 8 1/2″ × 11″ paper—not that sticky, erasable paper.

- Use the front side of the paper only.

- Staple once or clip in the upper left-hand corner.

- If you type on a computer, remove perforated edges.

Typeface

- If you have a choice, use pica (10 characters per inch) typeface.

- Do not use all-capital letters or all italics.

Spacing

- Double-space between lines.

- Use an inch to an inch-and-a-half margin on all four sides.

- Indent the first line of each paragraph five spaces.

- Do not justify (line up the margin) on the right unless asked to do so. Justifying on the right distorts the spacing between letters and words, making your paper harder to read.

- At the bottom of the page, use a full last line, unless you're ending a paragraph. It's all right to end a page in mid-sentence.

Spacing After Punctuation

- Leave *two* spaces after

    Periods
    Question marks
    Exclamation marks
    Colons

- Leave *one* space after

    Commas
    Semicolons

- Make a dash by using two hyphens—with no space before or after.

- Make an ellipsis (. . .) by using three periods with a space before and after each period.

- Never begin a line with a period or a comma.

- Never put a space before a punctuation mark.

Dividing Words

- Avoid, as much as possible, dividing words from one line to the next. If a word has five letters or fewer, fit it on one line or the other.

- Divide only between syllables. To find the syllables, look up the word in a dictionary. It will be printed with dots between the syllables: *guar·an·tee.*

- Never divide a one-syllable word, like *brought.*

- Never divide a word after only one letter.

Page Numbers

Number each page after the first.

Cover Sheet

- The title, without quotation marks or underlining
- Your name
- The date
- The course title and number
- The teacher's name

Center the title in the middle of the page and put the other information in the lower right-hand corner.

■ SOME ADVICE ABOUT TYPING

You'll need to hand in many typed papers in college, so it pays to learn to type or use a word processor. If you don't have a computer, most colleges and many public libraries have a computer room where you can take your own disk and type and print out your paper.

If, however, a friend or relative types for you, be sure that the typist doesn't interfere with the content. Don't let someone else tell you how to do your assignment.

■ A WORD ABOUT PROOFREADING

No matter who has typed your paper, you must read the typed copy several times. A typo counts as an error; it's no excuse to say, "Oh, that's just a typo."

Often teachers don't mind if you correct your typed copy with a pen. If it's okay, you can draw a line through the word you wish to change and write the correction above the line. Small corrections can also be made with correction fluid. If you use a word processor, proofread your paper both on the monitor and on the printout. Don't rely solely on a spelling checker; it will miss errors like *to* for *too*.

WRITING IN CLASS

A wave of panic—that's what most people feel when they are handed an assignment to be written in class. Some students, feeling the pressure, plunge in and write the first thoughts that come to mind. But your first thoughts aren't necessarily your best thoughts. There's a smarter way to write in a limited time.

Take Your Time at the Beginning

- Re-read the instructions carefully. Be sure you're writing what you've been asked for.

- Sit and jot down brief notes for a few minutes. Don't write whole sentences yet—just a word or phrase for each idea, example, or fact.

- Take a few more minutes to expand your notes. Stay calm. Don't start writing too soon.

- Decide on the parts of your essay.

For an Essay About Information, Stress Your Organization

- Write an introduction that indicates the parts of your essay. One simple technique is to give a full sentence in your introduction for each of the main points you plan to make:

Sigmund Freud is famous for three important ideas. He popularized the idea that we repress or bottle up our feelings. He explored the idea of the unconscious. Most important, he stressed the idea that our family relationships when we are children determine our adult relationships.

Note how the number "three" in the first sentence helps the reader to see the plan of the whole essay. Now each of these three points will become a separate paragraph in your essay.

- Write a paragraph for each point from your introduction. In each middle paragraph, restate the point, explain what you mean by any general words, and give facts or examples to prove your point.

- Write a brief conclusion, stressing what's most important.

- For *short essays on an exam,* each answer should consist of one long paragraph. Write a one-sentence introduction that uses words from the question and asserts your answer. Then, in the same paragraph, present three facts to support your answer, explaining one fact at a time. Finally, sum up your position in the last sentence of the paragraph.

For a Personal Essay, Stress What You Have Discovered

For a personal essay, you have many more options. While the three-point essay can get you by, it can easily become stilted and boring. In a personal essay, you need more room to explore your ideas.

- If you can't come up with a strong introduction at first, write your essay and then go back and write an introduction. You might discover a central idea through the process of writing the essay, and this idea can then serve as your introduction.

- If you're asked to write about a significant incident or event in your life, begin your essay by describing the event. Describe it *briefly,* using vivid details to bring it to life. Then use most of your essay to tell what you learned from this event or how it has changed you.

- If you're asked to give your opinion about a topic, you sometimes can use personal examples to support your position. Begin your essay with a strong statement, making clear in your introduction where you stand. Use the rest of your essay to argue assertively for what you think is right.

- Be certain to divide your essay into paragraphs. Make sure each paragraph is full of *specific* examples, facts, or details—use your own experiences, your own observations, and incidents you've read or heard about.

- In your conclusion, don't preach and don't fall back on overused generalizations. Say what matters to you or what you have discovered.

Here are some other tips to save time:

Don't Start Over

- Stick to your plan. If you get a new idea, use an asterisk (*) or an arrow to show where it goes.
- Leave room after each paragraph for ideas you might want to add later. If you are writing in an exam booklet, write on only the front side of the page so that you will have room for insertions.
- If you add or cut a main point, go back and revise your introduction to match the change.

Don't Pad Your Writing

Use a direct, no-nonsense style. Don't try for big words— they just lead to errors when you are under time pressure. Simply state your points and the facts to back them up, one step at a time.

Don't Make a Neat Copy

Copying over wastes precious time, and the copy tends to be full of slips and errors. Instead, put a line through an error and correct it above the line; use a carat (∧) for a short insertion, an asterisk (*) or arrow for a long insertion.

Don't Rush at the End

- Stop writing ten minutes before the end of the allotted time.
- Read your essay for content. Don't add to it unless you

find a *major* omission. Late additions usually create errors and disorganization.

- Proofread, with special attention to the second half of the essay (where rushing leads to errors) and to the very first sentence. Look for words like *to* and *too, then* and *than.* Check your *periods* to be sure you have no run-on sentences or fragments. Look carefully to make sure that you haven't left out any words or letters.

USING THE COLLEGE LIBRARY

When you are searching for information, there's no better place to begin than the college library. Familiarize yourself with all these resources.

Public Access Catalogs and Computerized Catalogs

Most libraries have their card catalogs on a computer and no longer keep the public-access card catalog up to date: use the computerized catalog wherever possible.

Books, media holdings, and reference materials are cataloged by *author, title,* and *subject.* If you don't have a specific author or title in mind, use the subject listing; but be prepared to look under several different headings.

Whereas most public and high school libraries use the Dewey Decimal System, most college and university libraries use the Library of Congress Classification System. This system separates all knowledge into twenty-one classes, each identified by a letter or letters of the alphabet, followed by numbers. These letters and numbers are the *call number* and are located at the top or bottom of each entry in the catalog. You need the complete call number in order to locate a book. It also helps to copy down the author and title.

Stacks

These are the rows of books that take up most of the space on every floor. In order to find a book you want, you have to have the exact call number. If the book's not there, you can ask at the circulation desk if it's checked out and, if it is, put your name down to receive it when it's returned. The library will notify you when it comes back in.

The Reserve Room

This is the section in the library where you go to check out, for a few hours or overnight, books and other materials that your teacher has put aside for the class.

Reference Section

Materials in this section are usually encyclopedias, dictionaries, bibliographies, and special collections of information. You can use them only in the library.

Periodicals Section (or Index Room)

Here's where you find annual indexes—in bound volumes and, more recently, on computers—to newspapers, magazines, and journals. *The Reader's Guide* and *The Magazine Index* list all subjects covered in popular magazines. *The New York Times Index* lists subjects covered in *The New York Times* each year. Other indexes are more specialized; ask the librarian for help. List the periodicals and pages you want and check the holdings file, the list of magazines your library carries. Often a magazine is available in a bound volume, or you can get a copy from the circulation desk. Many times, especially for newspaper articles, you will have to read copies on microfilm or microfiche.

Microfilm, Microfiche, and CD-ROM

A separate area houses microfilm, microfiche, and CD-ROM. Each slide, roll of film, or disk contains hundreds of pages of newspapers or magazines. Someone is usually there to help you use the machine the first time; after that, it's easy. You can make a copy of any page you want, often on the machine itself.

The Pamphlet File

Somewhere in every library is the pamphlet file (sometimes called the "vertical file" or "clip file"). In this file are housed years and years of clippings, accumulations of pamphlets—all sorts of information about any subjects the librarians thought important. This is an especially good source of information for material pertaining to local areas such as your state or hometown.

Media Section

Here you can see slides, filmstrips, and videotapes; listen to records or compact disks; look at slides under microscopes; and listen to foreign language tapes.

Typewriters and Computers

More and more libraries are providing typing rooms, complete with electric typewriters and, even more recently, computers on which you can type your paper. As more computers enter the scene, centers are being set up within the library itself where instruction in using the machines is provided.

Two Other Important Services

Interlibrary Loan: At your request, the library can obtain copies of books and photocopies of articles from other libraries.

Computer Searches: For a small fee, you can request a computer search in order to identify most sources about a subject field. Many libraries now also offer on-line hookups to various databases.

WRITING ABOUT LITERATURE

■ HOW TO THINK THROUGH YOUR ESSAY

When you are asked to write about literature, you will need to be certain of your teacher's expectations. Some teachers want a *summary* of your reading, in which you tell the main points of what you've read, followed by your evaluation. However, most literature teachers want you to stress an important idea about the reading and to demonstrate the details that gave you your idea.

Omit Plot Summary and the Author's Life

Unless you've been asked to, do not include a detailed plot summary which repeats all the points of the reading or the author's life story. Remember, the teacher already knows what the book says but does not know your ideas about the assignment.

Gather Your First Impressions of the Topic

Begin by freewriting about the question you have been asked or the topic you are considering: Write your first impressions quickly, without pausing, to get your ideas on paper. Do not worry about organization yet; don't even stop to re-read. After ten minutes, read your ideas, underline the most important, and write a sentence to sum up your main idea.

Re-read the Text

Search for evidence to support your main idea, and also for evidence that might lead you to modify it. The evidence could include incidents in a story or subtleties of style. Make notes as you re-read, and mark passages you may wish to quote.

65

Organize Your Essay

Do not merely follow the order of what you read. Look at your original freewriting, and revise your main idea if necessary. Decide on the parts of your idea and the order that will make them clear.

Use Evidence to Back Up Your Points

For each main point you make, explain which details from the reading support the point. In some cases, *briefly* quote the author. After referring to a detail or quoting a passage, always explain why that detail or passage supports your point.

Write a Title for Your Paper

The title should express the main idea of your paper, not just give the title of the text.

■ TECHNICALITIES

Titles

Underline titles of books, plays, television shows, magazines, and newspapers. Put "quotation marks" around titles of stories, articles, and poems.

Authors

Use the author's full name the first time you mention it. Thereafter, use the full name or last name—not the first name by itself.

Emily Dickinson wrote 1,775 poems.

or

Dickinson wrote 1,775 poems.

Identifying the Title and Author

Be sure to identify the title and author early in your essay, even if you've already done so in your title.

In "Because I Could Not Stop for Death," Dickinson . . .
"A Rose for Emily," by William Faulkner, is . . .
Freud's *The Interpretation of Dreams* . . .

Note carefully the punctuation in these examples.

Verb Tense

Use present tense to refer to the action in a work of literature:

The speaker of the poem longs for his youth.
Early in the novel, Elizabeth misjudges Darcy.

Crediting Your Source

- If you are quoting from only one source, give information at the end of the paper on the edition you used. List the author, the title, the city of publication, the publisher, and the copyright date. If you want to provide the original date of publication, put it immediately after the title.

  Fitzgerald, Zelda. *Save Me the Waltz*. 1982, New York: NAL, 1960.

- Directly after each quotation, give the page number in parentheses.

  The novel ends with a couple "watching the twilight" (203).

- For a poem (such as Coleridge's "The Rime of the Ancient Mariner"), give the line numbers.

  Water, water, every where,
  And all the boards did shrink;
  Water, water, every where,
  Nor any drop to drink. (119–122)

- For the Bible, give the title of the specific book, with chapter and verse.

  To every thing there is a season, and a time to every purpose under the heaven. (Eccles. 3.1)

- For a play (such as Shakespeare's *Antony and Cleopatra*), give act, scene, and lines.

  Age cannot wither her, nor custom stale
  Her infinite variety. (2.2.234–235)

- For more than one source, see "Documentation."

HOW TO QUOTE
FROM YOUR SOURCES

A good quotation demonstrates the point you are making.

Keep the Quotations Secondary to Your Own Ideas and Words

Each quotation should illustrate a definite point you want to make. Before and after the quotation, stress your point. Maintain your own writing style throughout the paper.

Don't Use Many Quotations

Too many quotations chop up your paper and lead the reader away from your points. Most of the time, tell in your own style what you found out. Instead of quoting, you can *summarize* (give the main points of what you read) or *paraphrase* (explain a single point in detail in your own words).

Keep Your Quotations Brief

Short quotations are the easiest and most graceful to use. Avoid using many quotations of over three or four lines. If you want to use a long quotation, omit sections that do not apply and use an ellipsis (. . .) to indicate the part you've left out. A long quotation should be followed by a discussion, in the same paragraph, of the points you are making about the quotation.

Introduce Your Quotations

Direct quotations should usually be preceded by identifying tags. Always make clear who is speaking and the source of the information.

Frances Bigelow says, "Our history is also our destiny."

69

Incorporating the author's name and any other pertinent information into your text will vary your quotations:

> Dr. Trey Porter, an authority on adolescent psychology, maintains that teenagers share a major fantasy: "They all dream of the day they will be free from parental control."

In any case, don't begin a sentence or a paragraph with a direct quotation without an introduction.

Incorporate Each Quotation into a Clear Sentence

Be certain that your quotations make sense, both in sentence structure and in content. If you use fragments of quotations, be certain that they are woven into complete sentences.

> Photographer Michael George states that "wasting film" ultimately saves a photographer time and effort.

Note that the three examples in this chapter illustrate three ways to lead into and punctuate a quotation.

WRITING RESEARCH PAPERS

Here it is again, that terrifying request from a teacher for a "research" or "term" paper. Don't be scared by the names of these papers. A research or term paper is simply a fairly long paper in which you set forth a point of view and support it with outside authorities—sources.

Here are some methods for keeping control of your paper:

Before Beginning Research, Freewrite About the Topic

To discover your preliminary main point, write what you already know quickly. Write nonstop for about fifteen minutes without thinking about organization. You can include the reasons you're interested in this subject and questions you'd like to answer.

Write a Controlling Sentence

Before searching for reading materials, spend some concentrated time and energy on writing one major sentence that will explain and limit your paper. (Teachers sometimes call this sentence a thesis statement or a topic sentence.) The whole point is to *limit* what you'll attempt to cover; otherwise, you will read yourself into a hole and never get your paper written. You may sometimes have to use two sentences, but try for one.

Pizza is the most wholesome fast food on the American market today.

Search for Supporting Information

The first step is to choose your reading. Go to the library and comb all the resources there. If your subject isn't listed, look under other related subjects. You can also ask someone who knows the field for suggestions about what's best to read. Look for recent articles. Check bibliographies in the backs of books. It can be exciting to follow the leads that you discover as you search for information. Also, don't overlook other sources such as

- Local organizations
- Interviews with experts in the field
- A visit to an institution
- Your family
- Your classmates
- Local libraries
- Businesses

Take Notes from Your Reading

After you've written down a few key questions, focus your reading on answering those questions. Remember that you want to gather supporting information, not copy other people's words. Be aware that you cannot write your paper while taking notes. These must be two separate steps.

- First, write down the details about your source that you will need for your *Works Cited* page.

  For a book: author, title, place of publication, publisher, and date of publication
  For an article: author, title of article, title of publication, date, and pages

  Keeping an index card for each source with all this information is a good idea; then when you type your *Works Cited*, you can simply shuffle the cards into alphabetical order.

- Next, take notes *sparingly* as you read. Take notes in phrases, not whole sentences. You will drive yourself crazy if you try to take down every word. It's best to read a number of paragraphs, then summarize them in your own words. Immediately write the source (author's last name and page number will do it). If a quotation strikes you as well said or interesting, copy it word for word and put quotation marks around it in your notes. Be accurate in noting the page number, since you'll need to tell the page where you found your information.

A word about photocopying material: If you find something very valuable, photocopy it to save time. But immediately write on the photocopy the publication information so that you don't forget where it came from.

- As you read, if you get an insight of your own, stop and write about it. Remember, this paper should be written by a human being—you—and you need to develop your own opinions and thoughts about your subject.

- After you've finished taking all your notes, go back over them and mark all the important points with an asterisk or with a highlighting pen. You might also find it helpful to make a brief outline or a short summary from each of your sources.

Discover Your Own Perspective

- After you have read and understood your sources, put your notes, books, and magazines aside in order to find your own position.

- Spend time freewriting or listing ideas until you know what you think about the topic.

- Go back to the sentence you wrote before you began your research—the controlling idea. Is this still your main point? If not, write a new one.

Organize Your Material

- Without consulting your notes, develop a short informal outline—all the major points you plan to make, put into a logical arrangement.

- Still without consulting your notes, just from memory, write a paragraph about each topic in your plan. Even better, write a draft of your entire paper without notes or sources.

- Now you can consult your notes. Read them and see which notes relate to the main points on your list. You may remember a main point you can add to your list. See if particular quotations and facts fit any of your main points, but don't feel you have to fit in everything you've found.

Now Write Your Essay

- Don't try for fancy words and long sentences. Tell what you know, stressing what is most important.

- Write to persuade. Remember that you are the authority. Your job is to convince the reader of your view of the topic. Use the facts you have found to back up your position; support your position with every sentence that you write.

- Anticipate the reader's questions and doubts, and respond to them ahead of time.

Incorporate Your Sources into Your Paper

- Avoid merely giving a part of your paper to each source you read; instead, give a part to each of the points you want to make.

- Select from your notes only the support you need for your own points. Eliminate material that does not pertain to your main points.

- Use your sources to expand each of your points. State each point and explain it with material from your research. Every time you use an opinion or fact, give credit to your source in parentheses.

- After presenting quotations or facts, make clear how they relate to the point of your paragraph.

Vary the Way You Use Your Sources

There are three major ways of presenting information: *direct quotation, paraphrase,* and *summary.*

- *Direct Quotation*

  This is the most common method—and the one most often overused in papers. Avoid relying too heavily on quotation by consciously using the other two methods of *paraphrase* and *summary.* Your paper should not be more than fifteen percent direct quotation. Direct quotations are best used for memorable or distinctive phrases.

  In direct quotation, you use the *exact* wording from your material and surround the words with quotation marks. Even if you use only a phrase or a key word, you must indicate that it has been taken from another source by placing it within quotation marks.

  The sections on "Quotation Marks" and "How to Quote from Your Sources" will help you with the correct form of quotations and will also give you ideas for varying your use of quotations.

- *Paraphrase*

  When you paraphrase, you take someone else's ideas or information and put them into your own words. Usually you paraphrase one statement, not more than a few lines, at one time. A good place for paraphrase, rather than quotation, is in telling basic facts: dates, statistics, places, etc. The pitfall in paraphrasing is that you can't half do it. That is, if you mix in some of the author's exact words, you must use quotation marks around them.

- *Summary*

  When you summarize, you take a substantial amount of material and condense it. You can summarize a long passage, several pages, a chapter, or even an entire article or book. Use summary when you want to acknowledge a conflicting idea or when you want to cover a related idea without too much detail.

Revise Your Essay

Copying over a first draft is not revising. Careful revision requires several steps:

- Take the time to make sure that you have written clearly—not in an artificial style.

- Be sure that each paragraph has one clear point and is logically connected to the paragraphs before and after it.

- Omit or move information that doesn't fit with a paragraph's main point.

- Look for places where the reader will need more information in order to follow your point.

- Check for smoothness leading into and out of direct quotations, paraphrases, and summaries.

Edit Your Essay

Use *Rules of Thumb,* Part One, to make corrections before you type, and proofread the final copy as well.

PLAGIARISM
(Cheating)

Penalties for plagiarism can be severe: failure of the course or expulsion from the college. Unintentional plagiarism is still plagiarism, so be careful and know the rules.

Plagiarism means *writing facts, quotations, or opinions that you got from someone else without identifying your source; or using someone else's words without putting quotation marks around them.*

To Avoid Plagiarism

- When in doubt, always give credit for a fact, quotation, or opinion taken from a book or other source. This is true even when you use your own wording.

- When you use a writer's wording—even a phrase—always put quotation marks around the writer's exact words.

- Write with your books closed. Do not write with a book or magazine open next to you. Don't go back and forth taking ideas from a source and writing your paper.

- Don't let your sources take over the essay. Tell what you know well in your own style, stressing what you find most important.

DOCUMENTATION

The word *documentation* means that you have added two elements to your paper:

Citations of Sources
List of Works Cited

■ CITATIONS

When you give citations in a paper, you tell specifically where you got a piece of information—in other words, the *source* you used.

When to Give Your Source

You must acknowledge in your paper the source of

- A direct quotation

- A statistic

- An idea

- Someone else's opinion

- Concrete facts

- Information not commonly known

Even if you *paraphrase* (put someone else's words into your own words) or *summarize* (condense someone else's words or ideas), you still must acknowledge the source of your information.

If a fact is common knowledge (George Washington was the first president), you don't have to give your source.

How to Use Parenthetical Citation

These days *footnotes* and *endnotes*—with little numbers above the lines—are used less and less. The current method is *parenthetical citation*. In this system you give your source in parentheses immediately after you give the information. Your reader can then find the complete source at the end of your paper in *Works Cited*.

The three most common citations are
   Author and page number
   Title and page number
   Page number only

Author and Page Number

Put the author's last name and the page number in parentheses immediately after the information:

(Waters 297)

Notice that there is no "p." and no comma.

In the text it looks like this:

The best olive oils "often have a greenish cast" (Waters 297).

If your citation comes at the end of a sentence, the period goes *outside* the last parenthesis. (Exception: With indented quotations, the period goes *before* the parentheses.)

Title and Page Number

Often articles, editorials, pamphlets, and other reading matter have no author listed. In such cases, give *only* the first distinctive word of the title followed by the page number:

A recent survey compared frozen pizzas for taste and texture ("Frozen" 330).

Page Number Only

Put only the page number in parentheses when you have already mentioned the author's name.

> Regina Schrambling says that the Tex-Mex flavor is "welcomed by most Americans" (125).

When possible, use this method of citation. Mentioning the author's name as you present information makes your paper more cohesive and readable.

Special Cases

● Secondhand Quotations

When you quote someone who has been quoted in one of your sources, use *qtd. in* (quoted in):

> Julie Wilson, who says her food is "fresh and honest," makes a blue cheese and pear pizza (qtd. in Claiborne and Franey 69).

In this example Wilson said it, although you found it in Claiborne and Franey.

Note that Wilson will not be listed in your Works Cited; Claiborne and Franey will be.

● Interview or Speech

If your source is an interview, lecture, or speech, include the person's name in your paragraph and use no parenthetical citation.

● Two Sources by the Same Author

When you have two or more sources by the same author, use the first major identifying word to indicate the title of the work you're citing.

> Claiborne prefers to chop the mozzarella rather than grate it (*International* 440).

or

> Some chefs prefer to chop rather than grate the mozzarella (Claiborne, *International* 440).

- Organization as Author

  Sometimes the author is an organization.

  According to the U.S. Department of Agriculture, one slice of plain pizza has 145 calories (22).

  or

  One slice of plain pizza has 145 calories (U.S. Dept. of Agriculture 22).

How Often to Give Citations

When several facts in a row within one paragraph all come from the same page of a source, use one citation to cover them all. Place the citation after the last fact, but alert the reader at the outset with a phrase such as "According to Janet O'Toole, . . ."

Do not, however, wait more than a few lines to let the reader know where the fact came from. The citation must be in the same paragraph as the fact.

Remember: You must give citations for information, not just for quotations.

Sample Paragraph Using Citations

On the following page is a sample paragraph so that you can see how various citations are used. (You will rarely have this many citations in one short paragraph.)

When the first pizzeria opened in New York City in 1905 ("Pizza" 490), it introduced the classic Italian pizza—bread dough covered with tomato sauce and cheese. Now, almost a century later, pizza is one of America's favorite foods. In addition to the classic version, pizza lovers can take their pick of thin or thick crust, all-white pizzas, vegetarian pizzas, or even more exotic experiments. For example, there is Tex-Mex pizza, a taste Regina Schrambling points out is "welcomed by most Americans" (125), and there is the French *pissaladière,* which adds fresh herbs, black olives, and anchovies (Child 151). Julie Wilson, a Utah chef who calls her food "fresh and honest," offers a high-brow combination: pizza made with blue cheese and pears (qtd. in Claiborne and Franey 70).

■ WORKS CITED

When you were gathering your material, you may have used a "working *bibliography*," a list of potential sources. However, now that you have written your paper and have seen which sources you actually did use, you must include at the end of the paper a list of Works Cited.

There are four major points to understand about a *Works Cited* page:

- List *only* those sources which you actually referred to in your paper.
- List the whole article, or essay, or book—not just the pages you used.
- *Alphabetize* your list of sources by the authors' last names. If no author is listed, alphabetize by the first main word in the title.
- Format is extremely important. Pay special attention to order, spacing, and punctuation.

  Put the author's last name first.
  Double-space the entire list.
  Start each entry at the left margin.
  Indent the second and third lines of each entry five spaces.
  Notice that most of the items in a citation are separated by periods.
  Put a period at the end of each entry.

Specific Entries

Book

Author. <u>Title</u>. City: Publisher, date.

Waters, Alice. <u>Chez Panisse Menu Cookbook</u>. New York: Random, 1982.

Article in a Magazine

Author. "Title of Article." <u>Title of Periodical</u> Date: page(s).

Schrambling, Regina. "Tex-Mex Pizza." <u>Working Woman</u> Feb.
1988: 125.

Article in a Newspaper

Author (if given). "Title of Article." <u>Title of Newspaper</u>
Complete date, section: page(s).

"Pillsbury's Pizza Unit to Be Sold." <u>New York Times</u> 18 Mar.
1988, Sec. D: 1, 7.

Encyclopedia

"Title of Article." <u>Encyclopedia</u>. Year of the edition.

"Pizza." <u>Encyclopaedia Britannica: Micropaedia</u>. 1986 ed.

Article or Story in a Collection or Anthology

Author of article. "Title of article." <u>Title of Book</u>. Editor
of book. City: Publisher, date. Pages covered by
article.

Cook, Joan Marble. "Italy: Myths and Truths." <u>Italy</u>. Ed. Ronald
Steel. New York: Wilson, 1963, 31–37.

Special Cases

● No Author Listed

Use the first main word of the title and alphabetize
according to that.

"Frozen Pizza." <u>Consumer Reports</u> May 1986: 327.

● Two or More Authors

Give the last name first for the first author only; use first
name first for the other author(s).

Anderson, Jean, and Ruth Buchan. <u>Half a Can of Tomato Paste
and Other Culinary Dilemmas</u>. New York: Harper, 1980.

- Additional Works by the Same Author

Use three hyphens and a period in place of the author's name and alphabetize the works by title.

Claiborne, Craig. <u>Craig Claiborne's New York Times Video Cookbook</u>. Videocassette. New York Times Productions, 1985. 110 min.

---. <u>New York Times International Cookbook</u>. New York: Harper, 1971.

- Pamphlet

Follow the format for a book. Often an organization is the publisher. Sometimes no author is listed.

<u>Browning Microwave Oven Cooking Guide</u>. Mahwah, NJ: Sharp Electronics Corporation, n.d.

Note: If the city of publication is not well known, give the abbreviation for the state. Use *n.d.* for *no date*.

- Radio or Television Program

Underline the title of the program. Give the network, if any, then the station call letters and city. Then list the date of the broadcast.

<u>New York and Company</u>. WNYC, New York City. 10 Apr. 1991.

- Videocassette

List the author or director and the producer, the release date, and the running time.

Claiborne, Craig. <u>Craig Claiborne's New York Times Video Cookbook</u>. Videocassette. New York Times Productions, 1985. 110 min.

- Interview

Give the person's name and position, the kind of interview (personal or telephone), and the date.

O'Reilly, Kevin [Owner, O'Reilly's Pizza Parlor]. Personal Interview. 19 Oct. 1992.

A sample of a *Works Cited* page follows. It illustrates a variety of sources and therefore is longer than you probably will need. The facing page identifies the category of each source.

EXPLANATIONS OF WORKS CITED

Book with Two Authors

Pamphlet, Unsigned; No Date

Cartoon in a Weekly Magazine, Untitled

Multiple Authors of Book; One Volume Cited

Videocassette (Use this form for audio or computer works)

Repeated Author; Same Author as Above

Repeated Author with First Citing of Co-Author; Newspaper Article

Single Article from an Edited Collection (Use this form for an essay or story in an anthology)

Magazine Article (Monthly), Unsigned

Organization as Author; Two Volumes with Both Volumes Cited; Organization as Publisher

Radio Program (Use this form for a television program)

Interview (Use this form for a lecture or a speech)

Newspaper Article, Unsigned

Encyclopedia Article, Unsigned

Magazine Article (Monthly), Signed

Book with a Single Author

Government Publication

WORKS CITED

Anderson, Jean, and Ruth Buchan. Half a Can of Tomato Paste and Other Culinary Dilemmas. New York: Harper, 1980.

Browning Microwave Oven Cooking Guide. Mahwah, NJ: Sharp Electronics Corporation, n.d.

Cheney, Tom. Cartoon. New Yorker 30 Jan. 1989: 69.

Child, Julia, Louisette Bertholle, and Simone Beck. Mastering the Art of French Cooking. Vol. 1. New York: Knopf, 1966.

Claiborne, Craig. Craig Claiborne's New York Times Video Cookbook. Videocassette. New York Times Productions, 1985. 110 min.

---. New York Times International Cookbook. New York: Harper, 1971.

Claiborne, Craig, and Pierre Franey. "Feasts Against Frost." New York Times 17 Jan. 1988, Sec. 6: 69–70.

Cook, Joan Marble. "Italy: Myths and Truths." Italy. Ed. Ronald Steel. New York: Wilson, 1963. 31–37.

"Frozen Pizza." Consumer Reports May 1986: 327+.

Gourmet. The Gourmet Cookbook. Rev. ed. 2 vols. New York: Gourmet, 1965.

New York and Company. WNYC, New York City. 10 Apr. 1991.

O'Reilly, Kevin [Owner, O'Reilly's Pizza Parlor]. Personal Interview. 19 Oct. 1992.

"Pillsbury's Pizza Unit to Be Sold." New York Times 18 Mar. 1988, Sec. D: 1, 7.

"Pizza." Encyclopaedia Britannica: Micropaedia. 1986 ed.

Schrambling, Regina. "Tex-Mex Pizza." Working Woman Feb. 1988: 125.

Waters, Alice. Chez Panisse Menu Cookbook. New York: Random, 1982.

U.S. Dept. of Agriculture. Nutritive Value of Foods. Washington: GPO, 1981.

PART THREE

PUTTING A PAPER TOGETHER

WHAT TO DO WHEN YOU'RE STUCK

Sometimes the ideas don't seem to be there, or you have only two ideas, or your thoughts are disconnected and jumbled. Sometimes it's hard to know where to begin or what shape your writing should take.

Here are some techniques used by professional writers. Try several—some are better for particular writing tasks. For instance, lists and outlines work when you don't have much time (in an essay exam) or when you have many points to include. Freewriting works well when your topic is subtle, when you want to write with depth. You'll find several techniques that work for you.

■ TECHNIQUES THAT WORK

Freewriting

In this method, you find your ideas by writing with no plan, quickly, without stopping. Don't worry about what to say first. Start somewhere in the middle. Just write nonstop for ten to twenty minutes. Ignore grammar, spelling, organization. Follow your thoughts as they come. Above all, don't stop! If you hit a blank place, write your last word over and over—you'll soon have a new idea. After you freewrite, write one sentence which begins, "The main point I'm making is . . ." When you've freewritten several times, read your writing and underline the good sentences. These can be the heart of your essay. You can make a list of them and toy with the order of your final essay. Freewriting takes time, but it is the easiest way to begin and leads to surprising and creative results.

Lists and Outlines

Before you write any sentences, make a list of the points you might use in your essay, including any examples and details that come to mind. Jot them down briefly, a word or phrase for each item. Keeping these points brief makes them easier to read and rearrange. Include any ideas you think of in one long list down the page. When you run dry, wait a little—more ideas will come.

Now start grouping the items on the list. Draw lines connecting examples to the points they illustrate. Then make a new list with the related points grouped together. Decide which idea is most important and cross out ideas or details which do not relate to it. Arrange your points so that each will lead up to the next. Be sure each section of your essay has examples or facts to strengthen your ideas.

You're ready to write. You'll see that this system works best when you have a big topic with many details. Although it seems complicated, it actually saves time. Once you have your plan, the writing of the essay will go very fast.

Working from a Core Paragraph

Write just one paragraph—at least six sentences—that tells the main ideas you have in mind. Arrange the sentences in a logical and effective sequence. Then copy each sentence from that core paragraph onto its own page and write a paragraph to back up each sentence. Now you have the rough draft of an essay.

Using a Tape Recorder

If you have trouble writing as fast as you think, talk your ideas into a recorder. Play them back several times, stopping to write down the best sentences. Another method is to write down four or five sentences before you begin, each starting with the main word of your topic, each different from the others. As you talk, use these sentences to get going when you run dry and to make sure you discuss different aspects of your topic.

A Relaxation Technique to Clear Your Mind

Sit up straight in a chair, put your feet flat on the floor, and place your palms on your thighs. Breathe very slowly, feeling the air spiral through your body. Focus on a spot on the floor. Feel each part of your body relax, starting with your feet. Take your time. Listen to the most distant sounds you can hear, the faintest sounds. Take several minutes or more being still, ears open, muscles relaxing, concentrating on your slow breathing. Then take a deep breath and begin to freewrite.

Talking to a Friend

The idea here is for your friend to help you discover and organize *your* ideas—not to tell you his or her ideas. The best person for this technique is not necessarily a good writer, but he or she must be a good listener. Ask your friend just to listen and not say anything for a few minutes. As you talk, you might jot down points you make. Then ask what came across most vividly. As your friend responds, you may find yourself saying more, trying to make a point clearer. Make notes of the new points, but don't let your friend write or dictate words for you. Once you have plenty of notes, you're ready to be alone and to freewrite or outline. If no friend is available, imagine that a friend is there and talk through your ideas.

■ TIME WASTERS: WHAT *NOT* TO DO

Don't Recopy Repeatedly

Get down a complete first draft before you try to revise any of it. Write on every second or third line so that you can revise easily. Keep a sheet of note paper handy to jot down new thoughts when they occur, and place a number or star to mark the places where you plan to insert new thoughts.

Don't Use a Dictionary or Thesaurus Before the Second Draft

Delay your concern for precise word usage and spelling until you have the whole paper written. Then go back and make improvements.

Don't Spend Hours on an Outline

You will probably revise your outline after the first draft, so don't get bogged down at the beginning. Even with long papers, a topic outline (naming the idea for each paragraph without supporting details) is often a more efficient way to organize.

If you use notecards, arrange them according to the paragraph topics they support, rather than copying them onto an outline.

Don't Try to Make Only One Draft

You may think you can save time by writing only one draft, but you can't get everything perfect the first time. Actually, it's faster to write something *approximately* close to the points you want to make, then go back and revise.

Don't Write with Distractions

When you write, you need to focus your brainpower and physical energy. You can be distracted by music, television, or conversation in the background or by being too uncomfortable or too comfortable. Such distractions waste time by diffusing your energy and concentration.

FINDING AN ORGANIZATION FOR YOUR ESSAY

The purpose of your paper is to convince the reader of your point. Your goal in organizing is to produce a sequence of paragraphs presenting your point one step at a time. But there are many ways to reach this goal.

Some people need an outline; others write first and then reorganize when they see a pattern in their writing. Still others begin in the middle or write the parts of their papers out of order.

No method is the "right" one. Some approaches are better for certain topics; some are better for certain people. Do not feel that you have to fit into a set way of working.

When to Use a Formula and When to Make Up Your Own Plan

Sometimes you are given a format to follow. Sometimes you can discover a pattern that you can repeat for similar assignments. For instance, lab reports often start with the question to be investigated, then describe the experiment to be tried, follow with your observations, and end with your conclusions. After doing one or two, you may be able to stick with a set pattern. A formula is especially useful for assignments you must do quickly. But for many topics you will need to discover the best plan by making lists of ideas and reordering them, or by writing for a while and then reworking what you've written.

How to Make Your Own Plan

Here's a method that works for many writers:

- Make a random list—written in *phrases,* not sentences—of all the ideas and facts you want to include. Don't be stingy. Make a long list.

- Now look at your list and decide which are your main points and which points support them.

- Write a single sentence or two which contain the major point you are going to make. Make sure that this point is stated early in your essay.

- Decide on the order of your main points. Sometimes you will want to put your points in *chronological* order— that is, in the sequence in which events occurred. Other times you will want to put them in *dramatic* order, building to the strongest point.

  Some topics lend themselves to particular arrangements. Here are a few:

  generalization followed by examples or arguments
  process (the steps for how something is done)
  comparison (similarities and differences)
  classification (types and categories)
  problem and solution
  cause and effect

- Cross off points from your list that do not fit the pattern or plan you are using. Remember, you can't put in everything you know.

- Decide on your paragraphs; write a sentence for each paragraph which tells what you plan to say.

- Now start writing. Get a rough draft finished before you reconsider your organization.

When to Adjust Your Plan

Sometimes the trick to good organization is *reorganization*. No matter whether you start with an outline, no matter what you think when you begin, your topic may well shift and change as you write. Often you will come up with better ideas, and as a result, you may change your emphasis. Therefore, you must be ready to abandon parts or all of your original plan. Some minor points may now become major points. Most writers need to revise their plan *after* they finish a first draft.

In the end, make sure that you know the main point you want the reader to get and that every sentence contributes to making that point clear.

HOW TO WORK ON A SECOND DRAFT

Revision is not just fixing errors. It means taking a fresh look at all aspects of your paper, moving some parts of it, and completely rewriting others. Look at your first draft from the following angles.

The Real Goal of Your Paper

- A big danger is straying from your subject. It's tempting to include good ideas or long examples that are related to your subject but do not support your main point.

- You might find it helpful to write a sentence that begins, "The main point of my paper is . . ." This sentence does not necessarily go into your paper, but keep it in front of you as you revise to make sure that every detail supports your main point. Notice that your *real* point may not be the point with which you started. As you look over your work, decide what you are really saying. You may need to write a new introduction that stresses your real goal.

The Order of Your Points

If you have trouble getting from one point to the next, you may need to omit one point or to move your points around.

- Make a list of your points in the order you wrote them.

- Now play with the order so that each one logically leads to the next.

- Get rid of points that aren't related.

- Cover some points briefly as parts of other points.

Make sure that the steps of your thinking are clear, complete, and logical.

Strong Parts and Weak Parts

- Build up what's good. When we revise, we tend to focus on the weak spots. Instead, start by looking for the good parts in your paper. Underline or highlight them, and write more about them. Add examples. Explain more fully. You may find that you have written a new, much better paper.

- Fix up what's bad. Now look at the parts that are giving you trouble. Do you really need them? Are they in the right place? If you got tangled up trying to say something that you consider important, stop and ask yourself, "What is it I'm trying to say, after all?" Then say it to yourself in plain English and write it down that way.

Reading Aloud to a Friend

- When you read your paper to a friend, notice what you *add* as you read—what information or explanations you feel compelled to put in. Jot down these additions and put them into the paper.

- Ask your friend to tell you what came through. All you want is what he or she heard—not whether it's good, not how to change it. Then let your friend ask you questions. However, don't let your friend take over and tell you what to write.

Final Touches

- Look again at the proportions of your paper. Are some of the paragraphs too short and choppy? Is there one that is overly long?

- Look at your first and last paragraphs. You may find that your old first paragraph is no longer your real point. If so, write a new one. Play with the first and last sentences of your paper in order to begin and end with the strongest statements that you can. For an important sentence, write the idea three or four different ways— with very different wording—then choose the best.

- Write a title that catches the reader's attention and that announces your subject.

- Proofread your paper closely several times and make corrections. Watch especially for errors in any of the new material you've written.

HOW TO MAKE A PAPER LONGER (AND WHEN TO MAKE IT SHORTER)

Adding words and phrases to your paper makes it at most an inch longer. Adding new points or new examples will make it grow half a page at a time. There are times, however, when cutting a little bit will make your whole paper stronger.

How to Make a Paper Longer

- Add an example or explain your reasons to demonstrate your point—or even add a new point.

- Mention other views of the subject that differ from yours: either incorporate them (showing the evidence for them) or disprove them (telling why others might accept them and why you reject them).

- Add details (facts, events that happened, things you can see or hear). Details are the life of a paper. Instead of writing, "We got something to drink," write "We swiped a six-pack from Tom's cooler."

- Expand your conclusion: Discuss implications and questions which your paper brings to mind

  BUT

- Don't add empty phrases, because they make your writing boring. Don't fake length by using fat margins, big handwriting, or a large typeface.

When to Make a Paper Shorter

- Condense minor points. Sometimes you think a point is necessary, but when you read your paper to a friend, you notice that you both get bored in that section. Or sometimes you get tangled up trying to make a point clear when you can cover it briefly or cut it entirely.

- Watch your *pace* when you tell a series of events. Head toward the main point or event directly. Don't get lost in boring preliminary details.

- Avoid getting sidetracked. The digression may interest you, but it may not add to the real point of the essay.

INTRODUCTIONS AND CONCLUSIONS

Beginnings and endings of everything, including written essays, demand special attention. After you've written your paper, pretend that you are a reader leafing through a magazine. Would you stop to read your paper? Would you lose interest at the end? You may need to add an introduction that snags a reader's interest or a conclusion that puts what you've written into perspective.

To get a memorable first or last sentence, try writing *five* sentences. They can express the same basic idea, but they should be worded as differently as possible—one long, one short, one plain, one elegant. If you write five, you'll find the one you want.

■ INTRODUCTIONS

In an essay exam or under time pressure, write the introduction first to indicate the map of the paper. In a longer essay, taking time with the introduction may trigger the whole essay and tell you what you want to say. Sometimes you may get stuck writing an introduction. In that case, try writing your introduction *after* you've written the rest of the first draft. Often you don't find your real main point until you've written several pages.

Here are a few common methods for beginning an essay:

Indicate the Parts of Your Essay

In academic papers and in technical or business reports, the introduction should indicate what is coming. Write a brief paragraph summing up the points you plan to make, one at a time. Then, in the middle of your paper, give each point a paragraph.

There were three causes of the sudden population increase in eighteenth-century Europe. First, the newly settled colonies provided enough wealth to support more people. Second, eighteenth-century wars did not kill as many Europeans as did seventeenth-century wars. Finally, the discovery of the potato provided a cheap food source.

Sometimes you can indicate the parts of your essay more subtly:

Although *Walden* and *Adventures of Huckleberry Finn* treat similar themes, the two books have very different tones and implications.

Take a Bold Stand

Start out with a strong statement of your position.

Millard Filmore is the most underrated President in American history.

Start with the Other Side

Tell what you disagree with and who said it. Give the opposing reasons so that you can later prove them wrong. For examples of this technique, see the editorial or "opinion" page of your newspaper.

Tell a Brief Story

Give one or two paragraphs to a single typical case, and then make your general point. The brief story makes clear the personal implications of the topic you will present. Magazine articles often use this method.

Move from the General to the Specific

Begin with the wider context of the topic and then zero in on the case at hand.

When we think of "strength," we usually picture physical strength—for instance, a weight lifter. But there are subtler forms of strength. Perhaps the rarest is moral strength: the ability to do what is right, even when it is inconvenient, unpopular, or dangerous. My grandfather in Italy was actually a strongman in the circus, but I remember him more for his moral strength than for his powerful arms.

Use the News Lead

Write one sentence incorporating *who, what, when, where, how,* and sometimes *why*

   During the fourteenth century, in less than three years, one-third of Europe's population died of the bubonic plague.

■ CONCLUSIONS

Don't end your paper with preaching or clichés. Consider, out of all that you have written, what is most important. Sometimes you want a quick summation, but other times you will have a longer conclusion that probes your topic more deeply.

Here are several approaches to writing a conclusion:

Summarize

Stress your main points, but avoid repeating earlier phrases word for word.

Suggest a Solution to a Problem

Come up with a solution you think might make a difference, and tell how the information you've presented could affect the future.

Put Your Ideas in a Wider Perspective

What is the importance of what you have said? What is the larger meaning? Move from the specifics of your topic to the deeper concerns it suggests.

Raise Further Questions or Implications

Which issues now remain? Acknowledge the limitations of what you have covered. Reaffirm what you *have* established. Examine what it implies.

PARAGRAPHS— LONG AND SHORT

The paragraphs of your essay lead the reader step by step through your ideas. Each paragraph should make one point, and every sentence in it should relate to that one point. Usually the paragraph begins by stating the point and then goes on to explain it and make it specific.

Paragraphs should be as long as they need to be to make one point. Sometimes one or two strong sentences can be enough. At other times you need nine or ten sentences to explain your point. However, you want to avoid writing an essay that consists of either one long paragraph or a series of very short ones. Paragraphs give readers a visual landing, a place to pause; so use your eye and vary the lengths of your paragraphs.

■ INDENT THE FIRST WORD OF THE PARAGRAPH

In college papers, indent the first word of each paragraph *five* spaces in typing, and approximately that amount of space if you are writing by hand. In business letters or reports, where you single-space between lines, omit the indention and double-space between the paragraphs to divide them.

■ BREAK UP LONG PARAGRAPHS

A paragraph that is more than ten sentences usually should be divided. Find a natural point for division, such as

- A new subject or idea
- A turning point in a story
- The start of an example
- A change of location or time

■ EXPAND SHORT PARAGRAPHS

Too many short paragraphs can make your thought seem fragmented. If you have a string of paragraphs which consist of one or two sentences, you may need to *combine, develop,* or *omit* some of your paragraphs.

Combine

- Join two paragraphs on the same point.
- Include examples in the same paragraph as the point they illustrate.
- Regroup your major ideas and make a new paragraph plan.

Develop

- Give examples or reasons to support your point.
- Cite facts, statistics, or evidence to support your point.
- Relate an incident or event that supports your point.
- Explain a general term.
- Quote authorities to back up what you say.

Omit

If you have a short paragraph that cannot be expanded or combined with another, chances are that paragraph should be dropped. Sometimes you have to decide whether you really want to explain a particular point or whether it's not important to your paper.

■ CHECK FOR CONTINUITY

Within a paragraph, make sure that your sentences follow a logical sequence. Each one should build on the previous one and lead to the next.

Link your paragraphs together with transitions—taking words or ideas from one paragraph and using them at the beginning of the next one.

■ A TIP

If you keep having trouble with your paragraphs, you can rely on this basic paragraph pattern:

- A main point stated in one sentence
- An explanation of any general words in your main point
- Examples or details that support your point
- The reason each example supports your point
- A sentence to sum up

TRANSITIONS

Transitions are *bridges* in your writing which take the reader from one thought to the next. These bridges link your ideas together and help you to avoid choppy writing.

First Check the Order of Your Ideas

If you are having trouble with transitions, it may be that your points are out of order. Make a list of your main points and juggle your order so that one paragraph leads logically to the next. Then add transitions which underscore the movement from one point to the next.

Use Transition Words

Keep your transitions brief and inconspicuous. Here are some choices of transition words you can use to illustrate certain points or relationships:

Adding a Point:	furthermore, besides, finally, in addition to
Emphasis:	above all, indeed, in fact, in other words, most important
Time:	then, afterwards, eventually, next, immediately, meanwhile, previously, already, often, since then, now, later, usually
Space:	next to, across, from, above, below, nearby, inside, beyond, between, surrounding
Cause and Effect:	consequently, as a result, therefore, thus
Examples:	for example, for instance
Progression:	first, second, third, furthermore
Contrast:	but, however, in contrast, instead, nevertheless, on the contrary, on the other hand, though, still, unfortunately
Similarity:	like, also, likewise, similarly, as, then too

Concession:	although, yet, of course, after all, granted, while it is true
Conclusions:	therefore, to sum up, in brief, in general, in short, for these reasons, in retrospect, finally, in conclusion

Use Repetition of Key Words and Ideas

- Repeat the word itself or variations of it.

  I can never forget the *year* of the flood. That was the *year* I grew up.
  Everyone agreed that Iona was *beautiful.* Her *beauty,* however, did not always endear her to others.

- Use pronouns.

  People who have hypoglycemia usually need to be on a special diet. *They* should, at the very least, avoid eating sugar.

- Use synonyms—different words with the same meaning.

  When you repot plants, be certain to use a high grade of potting *soil.* Plants need good rich *dirt* in order to thrive.
  Even though the woman was *handcuffed,* she kept running around, waving her *manacled* hands in the air.

Use Transitional Sentences Between Paragraphs

Usually the transition between paragraphs comes in the first sentence of the new paragraph.

Even though Hortense followed all of these useful suggestions, she still ran into an unforeseen problem.
Because of these results, the researchers decided to try a new experiment.

Notice that, in these examples, the first half of the sentence refers to a previous paragraph; the second half points to the paragraph that is beginning.

PROOFREADING TIPS

Proofreading deserves as much attention as your actual writing. Careless errors undermine what you have said, so make a practice of proofreading several times.

Here are some tips to help you spot mistakes.

Make a Break Between Writing and Proofreading

Always put a little distance between the writing of a paper and the proofreading of it. That way you'll see it fresh and catch errors you might have otherwise overlooked. Set the paper aside for the night—or even for twenty minutes— while you catch your breath. When you write in class, train yourself *not* to write up until the final moment; give yourself an extra ten minutes before the end of class, take a short break, and then proofread your paper several times before handing it in.

Search for Trouble

Assume that you have made unconscious errors and really look for them. Slow down your reading considerably, and actually look at every word.

Know Your Own Typical Mistakes

Before you proofread, look over any papers you've already gotten back corrected. Recall the errors you need to watch for. As you're writing *this* paper, take ten minutes to learn from the last one.

Proofread for One Type of Error

If periods and commas are your biggest problem, or if you always leave off apostrophes, or if you always write *your* for *you're*, go through the paper checking for just that one problem. Then go back and proofread to check for other mistakes.

Proofread Out of Order

Try starting with the last sentence of the paper and reading backwards to the first sentence; or proofread the second half of the paper first (since that's where most of the errors usually are), take a break, and then proofread the first half.

Proofread Aloud

Try always to read your paper aloud at least once. This will slow you down, and you'll *hear* the difference between what you meant to write and what you actually wrote.

Look Up Anything You're Not Sure Of

Use this book and a dictionary. You'll learn nothing by guessing, but you'll learn something forever if you take the time to look it up.

Proofread Your Final Copy

It does no good to proofread a draft of your paper and then forget to proofread the final paper. This problem crops up often, especially in typewritten papers. Remember: A *typo* is just as much an error as any other error.

With a Word Processor, Proofread on Both Screen and Page

If you are using a word processor, scroll through and make corrections on the screen. Use the spelling checker if there is one, but remember that a spelling checker will not catch commonly confused words like *to* and *too* or *your* and *you're*. You will still need to proofread your printed copy.

PART FOUR
WRITING WITH ELEGANCE

115

KEEPING A JOURNAL

Keeping a journal is one of the best ways to grow as a writer. A journal helps you put your thoughts and feelings into words, helps you overcome writer's block, and helps you develop your own personal style. You will also discover truths you didn't know—about yourself and about many topics. Some of your journal writing can later be developed into complete essays or stories.

Make your journal a record of your inward journey. Don't make it a diary—a day-by-day description of what you do. Instead, set down your memories, your feelings, your observations, your hopes. A journal gives you the opportunity to try your hand at different types of writing, so aim for variety in your entries.

Some Guidelines for Keeping a Journal

- Write nearly every day for at least ten minutes.

- Put each entry on the front of a new page with the day and date at the top. Fill the page and continue on the back if you have more to say.

- Use a notebook you really like. Write in ink.

- Choose one topic each day and stick to it. If you have no topic, write whatever comes into your head or choose one of the suggestions from the list given here.

- While you write, don't worry about correctness. Write as spontaneously and as honestly as you can, and let your thoughts and words flow freely. Remember, this journal is for *you,* and it will be a source of delight to you in years to come.

- After you've written, go back immediately and proofread and make corrections. Be certain you've said what you mean.

Some Suggestions for Journal Entries

Blow off steam.

Describe someone you love.

Tell your favorite story about yourself when you were little.

State a controversial opinion that you have and then defend your position.

Respond to a movie, a TV program, a book, an article, a concert, a song.

Write a letter to someone and say what you can't say face to face.

Describe in full detail a place you know and love.

Remember on paper your very first boyfriend or girlfriend.

Make a list of all the things you want to do.

Immortalize one of your enemies in writing.

Relate, using present tense, a memorable dream you've had.

Sit in front of a drawing or painting and write down the feelings and images it evokes in you.

Describe yourself in a crowd.

Analyze the personal trait that gets you in trouble the most.

Relate an incident in which you were proud (or ashamed) of yourself.

Describe your dream house.

Capture on paper some object—such as a toy or piece of clothing—that you loved as a child.

Go all the way back: Try to remember your very first experience in the world and describe how it looked to you then.

Make a list of your accomplishments.

Write down a family story. Include when and where you have heard it.

Re-create your favorite meal, food, or recipe on paper.

Set down a "here-and-now" scene: Record sensory details right at the moment you're experiencing them.

Go to a public place and observe people. Write down your observations.

Relate your most pressing problem at present.

Describe your very favorite article of clothing and tell why it means so much to you.

Analyze your relationship to food.

Write about an uncle or an aunt.

Take an abstract idea such as delight, grief, or pride, and write down very specifically what the idea means to you.

Explain exactly how to do some activity you know well. Use sketches if you need to illustrate or clarify your point.

Write about yourself as a writer.

Explore several possible solutions to one of your current problems.

Trace the history of your hair.

Take one item from today's newspaper and give your thoughts about it.

Commit yourself in writing to doing something you've always wanted to do but never have.

Explain how you feel about crying . . . laughing . . . fighting . . . singing.

FINDING YOUR VOICE

Often we write the way we think we're supposed to, with big words and fancy sentences. The writing comes out awkward and impersonal. But good writing has the feel of a real person talking.

To find your own voice as a writer, keep these questions in mind when you write:

Am I saying this in plain English?

Are these words that I normally use?

Am I saying what I know to be true instead of what I think others want to hear?

A great technique for developing your own voice is to read your work aloud. If you do it regularly, you'll begin to notice when other voices are intruding or when you are using roundabout phrases. In time, your sentences will gain rhythm and force. Reading aloud helps you to remember that, when you write, you are telling something to somebody. In fact, another good technique is to visualize a particular person and pretend you are writing directly to that person.

Good writing is *honest*. Honest writing requires you to break through your fears of what other people might think of you and to tell what you know to be true. Your readers will appreciate the truth, shared with simplicity by a writer who has given the topic attention and has decided what is important.

ADDING DETAILS

Details give life to your ideas. As you write, you naturally concentrate on your ideas, but the reader will best remember a strong example or fact.

Adding Information

If a teacher asks for "more details," you probably have a generalization with insufficient support. You need to slow down, take *one* idea at a time, and tell what it is based upon. You cannot assume that the reader agrees with you or knows what you're talking about. You have to say where you got your idea. This comes down to adding some of the following details to support your point:

- Examples

- Facts

- Logical reasoning

- Explanation of abstract words

Ideas are abstract and hard to picture. To be remembered, they must be embodied in concrete language—in pictures, in facts, in things that happened.

For example, here are three abstract statements:

Gloria means what she says.
The scene in the film was romantic.
The paramecium displayed peculiar behavior.

Now here they are made more concrete:

Gloria means what she says. She says she hates television, and she backs it up by refusing to date any man who watches TV.

The soft focus of the camera and the violin music in the background heightened the romance of the scene.

Under the microscope, the paramecium displayed peculiar behavior. It doubled in size and turned purple.

Adding Sensory Details

The best writing appeals to our five senses. Your job as a writer is to put down words that will cause the reader to see, hear, smell, taste, or feel exactly what you experienced.

You can sharpen your senses with "here and now" exercises. Observe and write exactly what you see, feel, smell, taste, and hear moment by moment. Expand your descriptions until they become very specific.

I see a loose wire.
I see that the wire to the right speaker isn't plugged into the amplifier.

I feel the sun.
I feel the sun hot on my back.

I smell food cooking.
I smell the aroma of garlic drifting over from the Spanish restaurant.

I don't like the taste of these potato chips.
The salt from these potato chips puckers my tongue.

I hear a noise.
I hear squeaky rubber soles coming down the hall.

This exercise will help build the habit of including careful observation in your writing.

RECOGNIZING CLICHÉS

A cliché is a *predictable* word, phrase, or statement. If it sounds very familiar, if it comes very easily, it's probably a cliché. Clichés are comfortable—often so old that they are in our bones—and they are usually true.

But because clichés are predictable, the reader loses concentration when reading them. In going over your writing, try to replace clichés with fresher, sharper descriptions.

Recognize Clichés

The best way to spot clichés is to make a list of all the ones you hear. Clichés fall into groups:

- Comparisons

Cold as ice	Slept like a log
Drunk as a skunk	Fought like a tiger
Hot as . . .	Smooth as silk

- Pairs

Hot and heavy	By leaps and bounds
Apples and oranges	Wining and dining

- Images

  Raining cats and dogs
  Up a creek without a paddle
  Your room is a pigsty.
  Between a rock and a hard place

- Sayings

  There are other fish in the sea.
  Read my lips.
  No use crying over split milk.
  Welcome to the club.

- Lines

  What's a nice girl like you doing in a place like this?
  Haven't I met you somewhere before?
  We've got to stop meeting like this.

- Phrases

  Madly in love   Ripe old age
  Easier said than done With bated breath

- "In" words

  Fantastic
  Awesome
  Wonderful

  This year's new expression is next year's cliché. (Try saying "groovy" to your friends.)

People use clichés when they have to play it safe—making conversation or writing for an unfamiliar teacher. Uncomfortable situations invite clichés—first dates, beginnings of parties, funerals.

Eliminate Clichés

- Often you can simply omit a cliché—you don't need it. The essay is better without it.

- At other times, replace the cliché by saying what you mean. Give the details.

- Look out for clichés in your conclusion; that's where they love to gather.

- Make up your own comparisons and descriptions. Have fun writing creatively from your own viewpoint and sensations.

ELIMINATING BIASED LANGUAGE

Biased language includes all expressions that demean or exclude people. To avoid offending your reader, examine both the words you use and their underlying assumptions.

Offensive Word Choices

Some wording is prejudiced or impolite or outdated:

- Eliminate name-calling, slurs, or derogatory nicknames. Instead, refer to groups by the names they use for themselves. For example, use *women* (not *chicks*), *African Americans* or *blacks* (not *colored people*), *Native Americans* (not *Indians*).

- Replace words using *man* or *ess* with nonsexist terms. For example, use *flight attendant* (not *stewardess*), *mechanic* (not *repairman*), *leader* or *diplomat* (not *statesman*), *humanity* (not *mankind*).

False Assumptions

Some statements are based on hidden biases. Look hard at references to any group—even one you belong to. Acknowledge that every member of the group does not believe or look or behave exactly like every other member.

- Check for stereotyping about innate abilities or flaws in members of a group. For example, all women are not maternal, all lawyers are not devious, all Southerners are not racist, and all Japanese are not industrious. Many clichés are based in stereotypes: absent-minded professor, dumb jock, Latin temper.

- Check assumptions that certain jobs are best filled by certain ethnic groups or one sex: For example, all nurses aren't women; all mechanics aren't men; all ballet dancers aren't Russian.

- In a pair or list, watch for inconsistency:

man and wife

Instead, use

man and woman   or   husband and wife

two Republicans, a Democrat, an Independent, a woman,
    and a black

This list assumes that everyone is a white man unless
otherwise specified.

Instead, use

three Republicans, two Democrats, and an Independent

Faulty Pronoun Usage

Check pronouns for bias:

Each Supreme Court justice should have *his* clerk make copies
    of the decision.

- One option for revision is to use *his or her*

    Each Supreme Court justice should have *his or her* clerk make
    copies of the decision.

- A more graceful solution is to use the plural throughout

    The Supreme Court justices should have *their* clerks make
    copies of the decision.

- Sometimes you can eliminate the pronoun

    A senior citizen can get *his* ticket at half price.

Instead, use

    A senior citizen can get a ticket at half price.

You can find more help with pronoun choice in the section
"Consistent Pronouns."

TRIMMING WORDINESS

Often we think that people are impressed by a writer who uses big words and long sentences. Actually, people are more impressed by a writer who is *clear*.

Cut Empty Words

Some words sound good but carry no clear meaning. Omitting them will often make the sentence sharper.

experience	proceeded to
situation	the fact that
is a man who	really
personality	thing
in today's society	something

In the following examples, the first version is wordy; the second version is trim.

The fire was a terrifying situation and a depressing experience for all of us.
The fire terrified and depressed all of us.

Carmen is a person who has a tempestuous personality.
Carmen is tempestuous.

The reason she quit was because of the fact that she was sick.
She quit because of illness.

Anger is something we all feel.
We all feel anger.

Get Rid of Being Verbs

Being verbs like *is* and *are* sap the energy of your writing. They dilute your sentences. Often you can replace *being* verbs with forceful verbs.

Look out for *am, is, are, was, were, be, being, been.*

Especially watch out for *there is, there are, there were, it is, it was.*

Go through your paper and circle all of these limp verbs. Replace them with dynamic verbs. This exercise produces a dramatic difference in any writing. Don't give up easily. Sometimes you will have to rewrite or combine several sentences.

There are three people who influenced by career
Three people influenced my career.

Michael was living in the past.
Michael lived in the past.

It is sad to see how depressed Mary is.
Mary's depression makes me sad.

His walk was unsteady.
He wobbled when he walked.

The woman is beautiful. Her hair is black and curly. Her eyes are green.
The woman's black, curly hair set off her mysterious green eyes.

Save *being* verbs for times when you actually mean state of being:

She was born on Bastille Day.
I think; therefore, I am.
I am bushed.

Avoid Redundancy—Pointless Repetition

He married his wife twelve years ago.
He married twelve years ago.

Be Direct

Tell what something *is,* rather than what it *isn't.*

Ron does not keep his apartment very neat.
Ron's apartment is a mess.

Replace Fancy or Technical Words

You can replace *abode* with *house* and *coronary thrombosis* with *heart attack* and bring your paper down to earth. Some subjects may require technical language, but in general, strive to use everyday words.

Don't worry that your papers will be too short: For length, add examples and further thoughts. Look at the topic from a different viewpoint. Add points, not just words.

VARYING YOUR SENTENCES

The same idea can be put in many different ways, and every sentence has movable parts. To get more music or drama into your style, try reading your writing aloud. When you come across choppy or monotonous sentences, use some of the following techniques.

Write an Important Sentence Several Ways

You can turn a sentence that troubles you into a sentence that pleases you. Instead of fiddling with a word here and a word there, try writing five completely different sentences—each with the same idea. One could be long, one short, one a generalization, one a picture, and so forth. Often you'll find that your first isn't your best. If you play with several possibilities, you'll come up with the one you want. This technique works well for introductions and conclusions.

Use Short Sentences Frequently

Short sentences are the meat and bones of good prose.

- They can simplify an idea.
- They can dramatize a point.
- They can create suspense.
- They can add rhythm.
- They can be blunt and forceful.

If you're getting tangled in too many words, a few short sentences will often get you through.

Remember, however, that you must use a period even between very short but complete sentences:

It was a rainy Monday. I was sitting at my desk. I heard a knock at the door. I waited. The doorknob turned.

Lengthen Choppy Sentences

Using *only* short sentences can make your writing monotonous. If you want to lengthen a sentence, the simplest way is to add concrete information.

Billy was popular with the girls.
Billy, with his slick hair and even slicker talk, was popular with the eighth-grade girls in the back of the school bus.

The book was boring.
The author's long descriptions of rooms in which nothing and no one ever moved made the book boring.

Combine Choppy Sentences

* One option is to combine two short sentences back to back.

Put a semicolon between them.

They wanted black; I wanted pink.

(Be sure each half is a complete sentence.)

Put a comma followed by one of these connectors:

but	and	for
or	so	yet
nor		

They wanted black, but I wanted pink.

Put a semicolon followed by a transition word and a comma. Here are the most common transition words.

however	for example	meanwhile
therefore	furthermore	nevertheless
instead	in other words	on the other hand
besides		

They wanted black; nevertheless, I wanted pink.
They wanted black; however, I wanted pink.

- A second option is to highlight the major point. Often sentences contain two or more facts. You can show the relationship between these facts so that the most important one stands out.

In these examples, two ideas are given equal weight.

I docked my sailboat, and the hurricane hit.

I love Earl. He barks at the slightest sound.

Brad lost a contact lens. He had one blue eye and one brown eye.

Here are the same ideas with one point emphasized.

Just as I docked my sailboat, the hurricane hit.

I love Earl even though he barks at the slightest sound.

Because Brad lost a contact lens, he had one blue eye and one brown eye.

Notice that the halves of these sentences can be reversed. *Because* can start either the first or the second half of a sentence. Other words that work the same way are *if, although, when, while,* and *whereas*:

Although she didn't study, she aced the exam.
She aced the exam although she didn't study.

If it rains Saturday, we'll have a picnic at home.
We'll have the picnic at home if it rains Saturday.

Usually the sentence gains strength when the most interesting point comes last.

● Another way to highlight one idea is to *insert* the gist of one sentence inside another:

Sheila makes a fine living as a model. She is thin. She has high cheekbones.

Sheila, who is thin and has high cheekbones, makes a fine living as a model.

The problem with most choppy sentences is that one after another starts with the subject of the sentence—in this case, *Sheila* or *she*. Sometimes you can use *who* (for people) or *which* (for things) to start an insertion. Sometimes you can reduce the insertion to a word or two.

I interviewed Nell Partin, who is the mayor.
I interviewed Nell Partin, the mayor.

Give Your Sentences a Strong Ending

The beginning is worth sixty cents, what's in the middle is worth forty cents, but the end is worth a dollar.

I walked into the room, looked around at all the flowers my friends had sent, took a deep breath, and collapsed into a chair in tears.

When the nights grow cool and foggy and the full moon rises after the day's harvest, Madeline, so the story goes, roams the hills in search of revenge.

What Louie received, after all the plea-bargaining and haggling and postponements and hearings, was a ten-year sentence.

To stress the most important parts of your sentence, tuck in interrupters or insertions. Put transitions or minor information into the middle of your sentence.

He argues, as you probably know, even with statues.

From my point of view, however, that's a mistake.

The interior decoration, designed by his cousin, looked gaudy.

Remember to put commas on both sides of the insertion.

Use Parallel Structure

Parallel structure—repeating certain words for clarity and emphasis—makes elegant sentences.

To be honest is not necessarily to be brutal.

Famous quotations are often based on parallel structure.

I came, I saw, I conquered.

—Julius Caesar

To believe your own thought, to believe that what is true for you in your private heart is true for all men—that is genius.

—Ralph Waldo Emerson

Ask not what your country can do for you; ask what you can do for your country.

—John F. Kennedy

Imitate Good Writers

Take a close look at the writings of some of your favorite authors. A good exercise is to pick out a sentence or a paragraph that you particularly like. Read it aloud once or twice; then copy it over several times to get the feel of the language. Now study it closely and try to write an imitation of it. Use the sentence or paragraph as a model, but think up your own ideas and words. This exercise can rapidly expand your power to vary your sentences.

POSTSCRIPT

You do your best work when you take pleasure in a job. You write best when you know something about the topic and know what you want to stress. So, when you can, write about a topic you've lived with and have considered over time. When you *have* to write about a topic that seems boring or difficult, get to know it for a while, until it makes sense to you. Start with what is clear to you and you will write well.

Don't quit too soon. Sometimes a few more changes, a little extra attention to fine points, a new paragraph written on a separate piece of paper will transform an acceptable essay into an essay that really pleases you. Through the time you spend writing and rewriting, you will discover what is most important to say.

■ AN INVITATION

Rules of Thumb was written for you, so we welcome your comments about it. Please send them directly to us:

> Jay Silverman
> Elaine Hughes
> Diana Roberts Wienbroer
>
> Department of English
> Nassau Community College
> Garden City, New York 11530-6793

If you would like to purchase individual copies of *Rules of Thumb* directly from McGraw-Hill, please call this toll-free number:

> 1-800-262-4729

ABOUT THE AUTHORS

A graduate of Amherst College and the University of
Virginia, Jay Silverman has received fellowships from the
Fulbright-Hayes Foundation, the Andrew Mellon
Foundation, and the National Endowment for the
Humanities. He has taught at Virginia Highlands
Community College and at Nassau Community College
where he received the Honors Program award for
Excellence in Teaching.

Elaine Hughes came to New York City from Mississippi
in 1979 to attend a National Endowment for the
Humanities seminar at Columbia University. She has
taught writing for more than twenty years—primarily at
Hinds Community College in Raymond, Mississippi, and
at Nassau Community College—and has served as a
writing consultant for a number of corporations. She is the
author of *Writing from the Inner Self*.

As Chair of the English Department of Nassau
Community College for six years, Diana Roberts
Wienbroer coordinated a department of 150 faculty
members and served on the Executive Council of
Association of Department of English. Besdes teaching
writing for over twenty-five years, both in Texas and New
York, she has studied and taught film criticism. She is also
the co-author of *An Easy Guide to Writing on the Computer*.

INDEX

Boldface numbers indicate the major discussion of a topic in entries with several page references.